Bipolar Shoes

People Do Matter

Dave O'Riordan

authorHOUSE®

AuthorHouse™
1663 Liberty Drive
Bloomington, IN 47403
www.authorhouse.com
Phone: 1-800-839-8640

Published by AuthorHouse 6/1/2012

ISBN: 978-1-4685-3636-2 (e)
ISBN: 978-1-4685-3637-9 (hc)
ISBN: 978-1-4685-3638-6 (sc)

Library of Congress Control Number: 2011963485

Bipolar Shoes is for everyone who lives with a mental illness. I am but one voice and hope to do some good for mental health by donating a portion of the proceeds of this book to the Canadian Mental Health Association.

I dedicate Bipolar Shoes to my family; they have always been there for me. I wrote Bipolar Shoes for my children and grandchildren so they could have some knowledge about bipolar disorder and its effects on me and to give them a history just in case.

I would like to thank the people who work in the mental health field, for their compassion and understanding. You have made a huge impact in my life your efforts are appreciated.

Anything's Possible

A few years back, I got into an argument with my wife Heather. She was fed up with me always complaining about everything, and dragging her down. I was in transition after moving from another province to start our new life together. Heather didn't get mad very often and I got her message loud and clear. She understood my frustration about not being able to find a job and challenged me to do something constructive with my time.

Even after being married and divorced three times, I still didn't get it. I shot my mouth off, boasting that I could write a story and get it published. Heather persisted on asking me what I had written. I sat in front of my computer and wondered what the hell I was going to write about. I would start typing, get about two paragraphs done and then delete what I had written, saying it was crap. I realized after doing this a couple hundred times that I was not getting anywhere. Although never one to give up on a challenge, I was frustrated and doubted my ability to complete this task, having no formal training in the art of writing.

I decided to start over and create a list of topics I could write about. I picked three subjects Golf, Soccer and Bipolar Disorder. Then I asked myself what I would be able to come up with for those topics. I chose to write a story about bipolar disorder. I was unsure where to begin. First, I wrote a page describing why I wanted to write such a story. That page became my introduction. Then before I knew it, I was telling my life story.

I felt emotion as I stroked the keys, typing with my two index fingers. I liked what I was producing and it made me feel good about myself. There were times when my emotions would get the best of me. I was crying one moment and laughing the next. I was able to be honest to a fault with myself and even though I didn't realize it at the time I was doing some deep inner healing.

I was able to understand and become more aware of my illness. I was now able to understand the effects my moods had on others. I was able to cleanse my soul by laying the foundation for a new beginning, and it felt great. I was consumed by this story, spending every spare moment at my computer writing. I knew I didn't have real expertise at writing but the story had flow, it was funny and it had an element of hope. I worked on this project for over two years. When I was done I had to decide what to do with it. I had a job and put all my energy into that. I printed copies of my story and distributed them to people I knew for their reviews. I even gave one to my boss as he was an avid reader. Of the fifteen copies I distributed I only had one negative response.

I decided to go the route of self-publishing. I named the book "Bipolar Shoes — People Do Matter." I dragged my feet a little and decided that since I had spent two years creating Bipolar Shoes I should have it copyedited to make it easier to read. When I received the manuscript back, I was horrified by all the red marks on it. I spent quite a while accepting all the corrections. I was pleased with the new look of the book and realized I had a long way to go grammatically. My story was good but my punctuation was brutal. I then decided to pursue a writing course.

I could never have imagined that an argument with Heather would lead me to write a book, but that's exactly what happened. I also realize that I wouldn't have a book published, except for my determination to complete the project.

In the end, I wrote Bipolar Shoes for myself. It was the best medicine I have had to combat this menace of an illness. I am a better man today because of this experience. I credit Heather for her determined support for me in all aspects of my book she is after all my number one fan.

Every once in a while a person can say he did something right in his life. I am now privileged to say I now have done two things right. Heather is my best friend, the only person that I can truly be myself with. She has made me such a better person and I can't imagine life without her. She is the best and the first thing I did right. The love we share is immeasurable and second to none. Bipolar Shoes is my second right thing. I say that because it helped me understand bipolar disorder and how it has hurt me with the things I have done. It's also allowing me to forgive myself. Knowing that my book could help other people learn to cope with bipolar disorder is rewarding. I have always lived my life with the attitude that anything is possible. Now I know it's true.

Foreword

By Jennifer Denton, R.P.N
Community Mental Health Nurse, Humboldt, Saskatchewan, Canada

I've worked with people with mental health issues for fourteen years. Most of my years were in the acute setting. Working the past four years in the community has proved to be interesting to say the least. A rural community in itself has its own struggles.

There are a few key facts that most people don't know about people suffering with mental health problems. People with mental illnesses have average or above average intelligence. Mental illness is not caused by personal weakness. These people are no more violent than the general population. On the contrary, they are more likely to be victims of violence. One in six people will be affected by mental illness. And the biggest obstacle still remains the stigma. The stigma hinders people from finding treatment.

Working with Dave has been a nice change. He can get a bit ornery at times, but we work well together! He is very good at recognizing when he needs a bit more help, when he needs to see the doctor or just have an appointment to talk some stuff out. I asked him once if he accepted from the very beginning what his diagnosis is. He said he thought he had, and it certainly answered a lot of questions about why he did what he did all those years. He said he always knew he was different, but just didn't know how. Working with Dave is a rarity in the sense that many people don't or can't accept what the doctors have told them. Being on medication and falling into this type of statistic is very hard for many to endure. It's overwhelming to hear and overwhelming to accept. Many people don't realize that their lives are not over; they just have hit a bit of a bump in the road. With proper care, exercise, eating, and sleep, often their symptoms stay under control for many, many years.

Recovery is a deeply personal and unique process. Even with the limits caused by mental illness, anyone can lead a satisfying, hopeful, and contributing life.

Many myths surround mental illness. Researching you or your family members' diagnoses is very important to understand what you will face. Being your own or your family members' advocate is very important. You need to speak up about what is happening with your care and your medication.

There are many famous people who suffer from mental illness—Winston Churchill, Napoleon, Agatha Christie, Beethoven, Einstein, and Robert Muensch, just to name a few.

Adjusting one's attitudes, feelings, perceptions, beliefs, roles, and goals can be a very painful process, yet often it is one of self-discovery, renewal, and transformation.

Everyone's journey is different. Use your supports; involve yourself in your care; be your own advocate.

Believe in yourself or your loved one. You have so many possibilities. However bad things may seem, it is possible to move forward. Nobody said life would be easy! They just said it would be worth it!

Introduction

I spoke to God last night while I slept, then asked the questions I've always had but always felt I'd keep to myself; our conversation went like this:

Dear Jesus, as I lay here in peaceful slumber, I can't help but think there is so much more I can do to help humankind. In the last few weeks, you have allowed me to partake in all aspects of your church again; for that, I am very grateful. However, Jesus, you know me better than anyone else; at this time, I need the guidance of God, yourself, along with the Holy Spirit, to achieve my goal to help people. I have a passion for mental illness; I am willing to take whatever steps are necessary to learn and help people in the same situation as myself. I believe I have the first ingredient, which is compassion. The second ingredient, which is passion, is something I wake up with every day. The third ingredient is the knowledge that comes from living with a mental illness for over thirty years of my life. No books can teach you these skills. The fourth ingredient is being patient; I believe if people have someone with understanding, compassion, and knowledge to talk to, it does make them feel better, if the person they are talking to does understand because he or she battles the illness him- or herself. I believe everyone has a story to tell, and mine is called *Bipolar Shoes*.

Mental illness treatment (in my opinion) is not a quick enough service in the healthcare field. There are not enough true professionals in the field to meet the demand. However, that said, I believe there could be a vital need for people like myself who have been through the process, been frustrated yet persevered because of our strength and belief in the system; I know we could help people until professional help is available. I want to be part of the solution to help people who are scared, frightened, or not sure of what is going on with them mentally.

I find myself in the hospital again with my illness. Once again, I feel the strong need for a psychiatric professional in our area. I think it's absurd to have to wait six months or more to get an appointment to see a psychiatrist and then to have to travel to see him or her. I am committed to being a vital part of this team and to work with people and gain their trust in knowing that I am going to do everything possible to help them.

I consider myself an expert on bipolar disorder, as I have lived and functioned with it for most of my life. I would love to share my knowledge with people who are similar and interested in making an effort to make mental health better in our community and in the world. Yes, I am but one voice; this is my life, the only life I know. Mental illness is an illness, not an excuse; I am living proof that you can lead a productive life while also making a difference.

I believe the time has come; with your guidance, God, Jesus, and the Holy Spirit, I know I can prevail. You once taught me that the strong must help the weak, that people will accept the work you do in the name of God, and that all people are your children. I believe in miracles, as I am still on this earth because of your grace. The miracle I want to achieve is making people in our communities and world more aware of mental illness—that it is not an evil thing, but an acceptable illness that can be treated and managed. I will commit the time along with the effort to make this miracle happen, to put my passion into helping the less fortunate as well as to educate them with my knowledge of mental illness. Hey, I'm Irish; I love to talk and fight. I liked to drink, too, but found it got me in too much trouble; I'll share all that with you later.

My motto lately has been "People Do Matter." I know that I was put on this earth for something special; maybe this is my calling. I don't think

I have ever been so passionate in regard to anything else. I'm not afraid of hard work or working for a cause; I believe fate happens for a reason. I have spent time in the hospital three times over the last few months, but not once have I had a visitor, nurse, or doctor that really knew what the hell I was going through.

I am flat ass broke, Jesus; I don't know how much longer I can cope with life the way it is now. I don't want to kill myself anymore; now, that's a good thing. You made me realize that was a bad plan, so I figured I'd write a book called *Bipolar Shoes*, an autobiographical story of my life. So, Jesus, you need to plug this book for me so my family can eat. Maybe you could talk to Bill O'Reilly and get him on my side; I consider myself the working person's Bill; I don't take any crap, either. I think Bill would make a superb president, and he certainly wouldn't do any "bloviating." Keep up the excellent work, Mr. O'Reilly; I enjoy watching *The O'Reilly Factor*. Maybe consider having Dennis Miller as your running partner and Geraldo Rivera as the attorney general; get rid of the pinheads and take proper care of our military.

Every time dumb ass celebrities make stupid comments about the US military, they should be fined big amounts of cash. I can't believe how they think; well, I'll tell you what I think: they should be put on the next plane out to Iraq and tell the men and women serving the great nation of America and our proud Canadian troops in Afghanistan what they think and then have a special survivor Iraq and Afghanistan series and see which one of the dumb idiots gets home alive. Let's see … making a movie: twenty million dollars; defending one's country, upholding human rights, dying for your country: common sense tells me it's priceless.

So, Jesus, I ask you to please guide me; I know you died on the cross to save us from our sins, and with your help, I would like to contribute to the wellbeing of humankind, as well as save some people who suffer from mental illness from unnecessary pain and torment.

I am neither a trained writer, nor a politician. However—oops!—I am an expert in divorce and bankruptcies. I will try to entertain and inform you, so sit down, and welcome to my universe. Make yourself at home as I give you my views of the world along with thoughts from my bipolar shoes.

Chapter 1

The Beginning of Me

The year was 1962, September 17 to be exact; my mother was yelling, "I don't want to have this child," as she was scared to death. Well, Ma, you did it; you gave that one last push, out I came, then you welcomed me into the world. Bernie and Pat O'Riordan were now the proud parents of me, David Michael O'Riordan, and we lived in Cork City, Ireland. Now, never ones to be shy, my ma and dad found themselves in the family way again the following year; my sister, Sandra Mary O'Riordan, was born on September 16, 1963. Needless to say, my new sister screwed up my first birthday party. I never got the traditional Guinness in my bottle, ha ha. Sandra turned out to be a terrific sister; we didn't fight much, as I knew she would beat the shit out of me at any chance and I would get blamed for it anyway. In 1967, my mom gave birth to my brother, Paul Gerard O'Riordan, a cocky little bugger who turned out to be very funny. Our family was now complete: no more kids, that is, but always lots of excitement.

My parents owned a fish and chip shop on Douglas Street in Cork called Kiely's. To be honest, I don't think I've ever tasted better (except for my granddads on Maylor Street, which was a close second and also called

Kiely's). I marvelled at my dad's ways. He was like the McDonald's of fast food in Cork; he built a fabulous business with his ways of thinking. He could remember all the orders. Friday lunchtime was the busiest time of the week; at that time, Catholics did not eat meat on Fridays, so the chipper was always packed. Dad would take all the orders, then recite them all back to the cheers of the crowd. His nickname was "The Brain Box"; it was great fun, a wonderful memory I'll always have. I'll never forget the smell of malt vinegar, the tradition of the chipper, and the sheer pride I had for my mom and dad for providing so well for Sandra, Paul, and myself.

I went to school at Christian Brothers Sullivan's Quay; frankly, I hated it. I still have issues about the punishment that was handed out. Now, don't get me wrong; I'm all for respect, but beating the shit out of a kid every day doesn't work, at least it didn't for me. I would have no problem shaking hands with the brothers who inflicted all those beatings with the leather, and I'd have no problem kicking them in the balls, either. Mr. Sullivan, you were ancient when I started grade two; you were the meanest teacher; well, it's a toss-up between you or Brother Sommers. Mr. Sullivan's nickname was "Fuzzy," as he only had a ring of hair. His favorite weapon was the wooden pencil box. Now, remember, we were only kids, eight years old, and that son of a bitch would give us two whacks on each hand for punishment.

Well, Mr. Sullivan, I hope God punished you before you got to heaven, like making you make a million pencil cases to replace the ones you broke, you miserable bastard. Oh yeah, remember that talk we had the first day I started school? You were right; butter doesn't melt in my mouth; it may have taken me thirty-five years to deal with this, but both you and Brother Sommers wrecked my childhood. All I can say is that I forgive you; I hope God remembers all the children you degraded, humiliated, and scared for life.

For me, personally, it's a shame that you were allowed to conduct yourselves in this manner. Just think of the minds you ruined and the people you shamed. I hope they have the UFC (Ultimate Fighting Championship) in heaven; you have about forty years to train, and then I'm going to put a beating on both of you. Brother Sommers, bring your leather; Fuzzy, bring your pencil box; I'll shove your heads so far up your asses you will smell your tonsils. Okay, tough guys!

Other than those two pricks in the roses, school was pretty good. I enjoyed learning. I was intrigued by Irish history and the accordion and sports, of course. I had a passion for hurling and Gaelic football, both national games of Ireland; my biggest passion was football (soccer in North America). I had a ton of friends at school: Christy and Jerry O'Sullivan, no relation to that bastard mentioned above; there was Tony Cove, Finbarr Ahern, Eddie Thornhill, Jim Morrison, just to name a few. I learned how to be tough at this school. Mr. Maroney and Brother Rogers were good teachers who thought instead of bullied; I respect them for that. It was a pleasure to also have many other fine teachers at that time in my life.

Cork City was a wonderful place to grow up. I had lots to do and lots of freedom to do as I wanted. Roche's installed an escalator in their store in the late sixties, and the lads and I would have great fun riding it over and over till we got kicked out: that was big in Cork in the sixties. My granddad's chipper, Kiely's, was located down the block, so I would pop in and say hi to him as well as my uncles, Matt and Martin. It was always a laugh a minute; even though I was only eight or ten, I always felt like a man and, of course, always had a full belly when I left there.

Every second Saturday, I would spend the night at my Nan and granddad's. I was about ten. Nan would give me smokes; she was cool. She had a mouth on her like a sailor's—never mind the farts out of her, which would make you swear a train was passing by. I had a very special bond with my Nan; I loved her but felt sorry for her a lot. She had had a tough life looking after my uncle Noel, who was in a wheelchair from a young age. It was hard work for her; she was a recluse and liked her Murphy's stout and paddy whiskey. We always had a laugh. I know that's where I developed the bad language that is with me to this day. I was ten when my sister and brother saw me on the bus with a cigarette; of course, they told Dad. When I came home at lunchtime, I was crucified; then off we went to the shop where I bought the smoke. The old man started giving Mrs. Monahan supreme shit; I never saw my dad's face that red. He wasn't done yet. I told him that Nan also gave me smokes, and I thought he was going to have a heart attack. Dad was pissed off. I had never seen him get that mad before; my ears were ringing for weeks.

Sunday morning would always consist of breakfast, having a wash, and getting some change from Granddad; then he would put Brillcream in my hair and again I felt like a man. Then we went to mass and then to the pub for an hour and back home for Sunday dinner. I had this routine every second week; Sandra would do the other weekend.

Some kids idolized football players or rock stars or famous people. I idolized my father. For me, the sun shined out of his arse, and he played a mean bugle with that arse, too. My dad was a bit of a prick when I was a kid, but I took the time to understand him and his logic. He didn't have much of a home life himself. My dad was the fourth child in a family of six children. His father was an alcoholic and abusive; the family often went hungry and had no money. My dad would never let that happen to Sandra, Paul, or myself.

I recall my dad giving me a crosser (crossbar) on the bike up to Granny Riordan's on a Friday with fish and chips for us to have for lunch. Then my uncle Donal would play the guitar or accordion, and we would have a singsong. I always loved those days. Granny dropped dead of a heart attack while out with two of my cousins; they were shopping downtown. I was pretty young and really don't remember her much.

What I do remember about that time, though, was looking in the mirror and finding out that I had two eyes that were in love with each other; yes, I had crossed eyes, and they looked bad. Mom and Dad spent time researching what to do, and I had corrective surgery at the age of eight. My eyes have been perfect ever since.

I always remember being at the Merries (amusement park) out in Kinsale with the family. Dad, Sandra, and I were sitting on a bench and this man walked by and Dad got up and followed this man. They had a brief conversation, and when Dad returned, I asked him who the man was, and he said that was his dad. That was the only time I saw my grandfather; I never met him, never talked to him. My dad put aside their differences and went to see him every day in the hospital till he finally died a horrible death; none of his other five kids ever went to see him. What compassion, what love, what a role model I chose to idolize.

My dad was well known around Cork as one of the best goal keepers; it always made me proud to see him play, and I would always get my picture taken with the team. Dad had very humble beginnings: he had a grade six education, but a smarter man I've never met. He was always full of dreams, always thought big, and always maintained the lifestyle he enjoyed. The family went on a holiday every year; my mom wasn't too keen on flying, so we would travel around Ireland. Then, in 1972, we were going to the Jersey Islands. Dad had convinced mom to try flying. It was an adventure for all of us, and we had a great holiday. To add to Mom's stress, I was bitten by a dog named Panda the evening we were leaving. Panda, a miserable menace, got me on my bike, and I got him with my Hurley a couple of months later.

In 1973, we traveled to Majorca, Spain; the night before that trip, I stepped on glass and had to get a few stitches. I couldn't swim for the first week; the tetanus shot I had gotten made me very stiff. It was a great adventure, seeing a new culture; we were treated like kings at the hotel. One thing that stands out for me in that hotel, though, was this Spanish gardener, a very nice man who spoke very little English and who always had a laugh with the three of us kids. Mom and Dad were relaxing by the pool while the gardener was spraying us with the hose. All of a sudden, this well-dressed man riding a horse started yelling at the gardener then pointing him off; it was the owner of the hotel. He did not approve of the gardener's actions. Dad went over to explain the situation to the owner; the gardener kept his job. That man was on his knees thanking my dad; he gave him a handmade leather wallet before we left. Then there was the day Dad called a cab. The driver did a U-turn to pick us up then got pulled over by the police; he got a hefty fine and was devastated. When we got to our destination, my dad paid the fare as well as the fellow's fine for him. It took me a lot of years to understand that it's not what you have; it's what you do with what you have. I learned more from my dad on both of those trips. Sure, I remember the sights and the stuff we did. I never forgot those kind gestures, along with the gratitude of those people for my dad doing what he thought was right.

School was now going well for me. I had Brother Rodgers as a teacher. I was enjoying the creativity he was seeking; he allowed us to express our opinions; he was firm but fair. I was on the school team for both hurling and Gaelic. I was passionate about the accordion. I could not read the music but could play by ear, a God-given talent that I have. I struggled a lot with reading, as I didn't like it; I had a hard time comprehending. I didn't like to handwrite; I preferred to print. I always enjoyed reading the paper. Brother Rodgers started a Saturday club for speaking Irish; we would talk only Irish while playing games, singing songs. It was good fun; school was now fun to go to.

In April 1974, my granddad Kiely had a massive heart attack and died while watching a cartoon. He was sixty-nine years old. It was an awful shock for Nan; she took the loss very hard. They were pretty close to their fortieth anniversary; even though they didn't show affection, you could tell they were very close. It was my first experience at a funeral, and it was sad for me to see everyone in tears. I felt so helpless for my Nan. There was nothing I could do but hold her hand and be the boy she would expect me to be. My Nan was a beautiful person whom I loved and admired very much. She would need me more than ever now; I would take my uncle Noel in the wheelchair and go for walks. I left him on the side of the road or in the middle of the road a couple of times as he barked at dogs, big feckin' dogs, then shouted, "David, David, come back here!" He knew I was scared shitless of dogs. I had the Panda episode, and then I had some big black lab lock on to my leg and start humping; I guess he liked me, but he, too, scared the shit out of me. Not many people know that story; yes, I had my leg humped, and no, he didn't finish. Noel was a character who loved football; we went to the matches all the time with my dad and Martin. It was good as we got right on the field because of Noel being in a wheelchair. He would give out constantly to the refs, the other teams' players, but everyone knew Noel. He was a definite character who didn't give a shit what he said to anyone, and he would do anything for a laugh. Most people couldn't understand him anyway, as his speech was not that good. Noel was a very intelligent man who was very funny and understood and accepted his disabilities, even though he didn't like them; it was all he knew.

For our holidays in 1974, Mom and Dad decided to go to Canada, Edmonton to be exact, as Dad had lived in Canada back in the fifties and always longed to go back. We had a month-long stay ahead of us and we were all looking forward to the trip. We arrived in Edmonton in early May and stayed with Dad's friends, the Varvas family: Mr. Varvas (Chris) and his wife, Barbara; daughter, Didi; and son, Billy. The Varvas family opened their home to us and made us feel so welcome. It was hard, at first, as we didn't know each other, but we were like family in a matter of hours. Chris owned and operated the Nite and Day Café on 118th Avenue in Edmonton, and we went there quite often. We went to Banff, and Sandra fell down a cliff behind the motel and broke her arm; she spent the night in the hospital. It was her turn for some misfortune as I had had it the last couple of years. We had a wonderful holiday and made new friends in Canada: the Cove family and the Rasmussens. Canada was awesome; we all loved it; we were in Edmonton for Klondike days. That was exciting to this twelve-year-old Irish kid; I had never seen anything like it; I thought it was brilliant. We saw and did so much that I could write another book.

We flew back to Ireland, sad to be leaving but glad to be going home, too. When we got back to Cork, it wasn't long after that Mom and Dad made the decision to immigrate to Canada. Sandra had asthma, and that was the only thing holding up the process. We were approved by the Canadian embassy and would have our papers within a few weeks. Arrangements were made for us to leave on December 11, 1974; it was about three months before we were to leave.

I would drop in on Nan every day after school; pick up her messages, and just visit. As the day got closer, my heart got heavier: here we are, going to Canada, and who's going to take care of her? It was the week before we were to leave; it was hard for me, knowing that I was leaving; I felt as if I was betraying her. The day we were leaving was one of the hardest days of my life. I was twelve years old, feeling like a man, when she gave me a hug and kiss and said we would never see each other again and that she loved me. Nan was right; she died in her sleep in September 1976. I still miss you, Nan; thank you for helping me write this. You are always in my heart, and I thank you for your love. I have such fond memories of us. Hey, remember: what goes through a hole fifty miles an hour? A rabbit on a Honda. It's a dumb joke, but I always see us laughing when I think or tell that joke. I always had fun at your house; it was always full of laughter, and man, as a twelve-year-old boy, I sure gained on my vocabulary. I will never forget you; I love you, Nan.

We arrived back in Canada on December 11, 1974, now as immigrants to a new country. Canada would now be home to us, and we would call Edmonton home. My dad had promised us snow would be on the ground when we arrived, but there was none. It was an unusually mild winter, they said. I will never forget the Christmas lights on all the houses; it was magic. We took the bus when we went out, as dad didn't have a car yet. My brother Paul decided to lick the ice at the bus shelter. He would have been almost eight; all we heard was "Ah ah ah," and the old man pulled him by the scruff of the neck. A good chunk of Paul's tongue was left on the shelter, and he was bleeding as we got on the bus. Paul and I got a couple of hockey sticks from the Coves; we would rip pucks at one another on the basement floor, no pads or helmets, just rip and shoot. We Irish were tough little bastards; we played hurling; how hard would it be? After several welts, numerous holes in the walls, not to mention the black marks all over the floor, we switched to a tennis ball.

Dad got a car a couple of days before Christmas, and I will always remember this: it was Christmas Eve, and we were on the Fort Road. There was an accident; a body was covered on the road; the police and ambulance were on the scene. Every year, I think of the family that person left behind and say a prayer for them.

I had a somewhat normal life in Ireland, but I was not really prepared for the culture shock here in Canada. My first day of school, I was scared shitless. I knew no one, and there were girls in my class (a first for me, as schools in Ireland were separate: boys in one, girls in another). My school was St. Gerome's; my teacher's name was Mr. Forest; he was the nicest teacher I ever had 'till that point. He did not like me calling him "Sir"; he said it made him feel old. I didn't know how to take this, as I always had to address my teachers as "Sir" or "Brother" in my last school. I had built a reputation back in Ireland as a good friend; I missed my buddies lots. It was hard; everyone laughed when I spoke because of my accent, so I would not ask questions. I didn't like everyone laughing at me. Of course, I had a temper and would fight the fellows bothering me about my accent.

I would ask the teacher after school for explanations; however, school was much better, as I never got the leather. I hung out with a couple of guys who were really nice, but at that time, we had nothing in common. They would be talking hockey, sharpening skates, taping sticks or complaining about dumb ass referees: something I knew nothing about and could not relate to. That would soon change; my dad was working at Burns Meat Packing Plant on the afternoon shift, three to eleven-thirty; we didn't see him much during the week, but lots on the weekend. Saturdays consisted of going for groceries, being home by three to watch Stampede wrestling and later Hockey Night in Canada. We all took a liking to the Toronto Maple Leafs; once we learned the game, we were hooked. I knew every player's name as well as jersey number. I was now very passionate about hockey.

We did not get any coverage of soccer here. They showed a German soccer game every week on PBS; we did watch it. I remember walking to school one day when it was really cold out; I did not have long johns on; I didn't even know what they were. I thought I was going to freeze my balls off or die; I had never felt such cold. Snow and cold were new to me; I didn't like either. I had been in Canada for four months now, but I really wanted to go home. My mom and dad would say, "You are home; you will get used to it." I missed my Nan, too. When I was thirteen, I got my first job as a busboy in the Varvas's restaurant, the Coliseum Steak and Pizza, which replaced the Nite and Day Cafe. When I got my first cheque, I went in the bathroom to look at it again. It was for seventy-eight dollars; man, I thought I was a millionaire. School was going well now. I still didn't study or do homework, but I was having fun. St. Nicholas was the school I now attended, a junior high. I used to give the teachers fits; I turned out to be the class clown, pulling all kinds of pranks. One teacher in particular would still have fits to this day if he heard my name; that would be Mr. Simmons. I used to take bets on how many times I would fall off my chair. The most I did was sixteen in a forty-minute period. People in my class could not believe I would do it; I could not believe I would get away with it.

In the same teacher's class, the fellow sitting next to me was annoying me, and the next thing I knew, this guy smoked me right on the forehead. Mr. Simmons, who was writing on the blackboard, turned around then asked what was going on. I said, "Nothing, sir." When he turned around to resume writing, I stood up, then drove Chris Plamondon with a left that I'm sure had him seeing stars. Mr. Simmons turned around again as Plamondon was composing himself. Our next class was gym; I no sooner got in the locker room than Plamondon jumped me. We battled for a while, then I hammered on him. Our next class was with Mr. Simmons again. He asked where Plamondon was; no one knew. It was about five minutes later when he showed up. Mr. Simmons said, "Now I can see you boys have settled your differences." Mr. Simmons used to call me "Father O'Riordan" in religion class; because I knew so much about the mass, he said I should be teaching it. The brothers beat it into me; I guess that's how I knew so much. I was starting to lose my Irish accent by now. I got tired of fighting, ha ha.

I remember one day when I was staring off, looking at the hills in the middle of class, Mr. Simmons got my attention. I was staring at Robin Yonkus; she had the best hills in the class; hell, they were mountains. I was getting interested in girls now. Mr. Simmons decided to give me a talk. He took me back to his back office where he grew drugs or plants or whatever, and he grew lots of stuff. He started giving me this talk: "Your parents probably haven't talked to you about this, as Irish people are scared to talk about sex." I was thinking, "Oh shit, how am I going to get out of this?" "How old are you now, fourteen or fifteen?" he asked. I answered fourteen, so then he asked, "Do you masturbate?" I said, "No, sir, not since I found a better place to put it." Our talk was quickly over and I was on my way; I was such a bullshitter.

I was playing soccer with the peewees when they realized I was a couple of months too old. By that time, the bantam team was already picked, so I couldn't play. However, they were looking for a coach for the mini mites, so I volunteered; they were hesitant at first but let me do it. I had a meeting with the parents to explain the situation that I didn't drive, so if they wanted the kids to play, they would have to pitch in and help. I got lots of support, Sandra helped me out as an assistant coach, and we ran drills two nights a week with one game for sure. With the work, dedication, and teaching, we had a very strong team after a few weeks; the kids were enjoying themselves. Sandra and I worked hard; we dedicated the season to motivating these children to understand the game and how it should be played. I had no issues with parents until the end of the year. We had won some money selling tickets, and the parents wanted to buy trophies for the kids. I disagreed and wanted each kid to have a good ball, and that's what he or she got. I was named coach of the year along with Sandra, and I was very proud of our accomplishments as a team. Paul was picked as the player contributing the most with the least recognition on his team; he was very excited by that honor.

When I was fifteen, I was diagnosed with a rare skin disorder called Darier's disease. It is where the skin sheds too fast. Dead skin flakes then create deposits; it itches, gets sore and is very uncomfortable. The hardest thing about it is not to scratch. I was very self-conscious about it. I thought everyone was looking at me or talking about me. I was embarrassed to go out with girls, but I dealt with it. I have often said to people, "What would you do if you had a couple hundred ants crawling over you; what would you do?" I deal with this every day. This was the same age when I started having unrealistic goals; I was working at McDonald's now, making lots of friends. I hated working there at first; all my school friends used to tease me. I was a year older than most of the kids in school. I got my revenge, though, the following year, when the same people who teased me started working there. By that time, I was a crew chief, so I was their supervisor. I have always taken a leadership role in everything I have done. I usually succeed. I take the bull by the horns and go with it. My first goal was to become an assistant manager, which I did at age seventeen; then I figured, why not own the place? Of course, that never happened. I always wanted to be boss, and I guess I always have been, in one form or another.

I met my first love in school; her name was Rosemarie Normandeau. When I asked her out on a date, she turned me down, saying we were friends; she was a beautiful person, and we did stay friends, but I was devastated at the same time.

The most enjoyable experience I had in school was band. I played the trombone; I picked that instrument because I thought it would be easy, but I was wrong; it's hard to play, but I stuck with it. My best friend in school, Glenn Tardif, played the trumpet. We ruled the class; you never knew what we were going to do next, but it was all in fun. Our teacher in grade eight was Mr. Sime. One day, he left the room, so I decided to load his chair with thumbtacks. He arrived back in class a few minutes later, and then we resumed playing. Tardif and I were up to our usual antics with a few of the other lads—Mick McElleney, Cubba (Calvin Viola)—and Mr. Sime kept us after class. He was quite pissed off at all of us, giving us shit, then he decided to have a seat at his desk. Man, I think he gave NASA new ideas, because it was a perfect launch; all we heard was "Holy shit" as he went about ten feet straight up, picking tacks from his ass. There were five of us rolling on the floor; three guys didn't know what had happened. To be honest, Glenn and I had forgotten we did it. Mr. Sime got beet red and even more pissed off; we were lucky he didn't beat the shit out of us. I did get my only A in English, describing the above story in an essay for a teacher called Mrs. Leeman who taught me language arts in grade eight.

In grade nine band, we had a new teacher named Mr. Ochoa; he was a short Philippine man with a good sense of humour who was very dedicated to the program. He was a breath of fresh air and just what our school needed. We did some magic with him leading us; we got into jazz bands with other schools. Mr. Ochoa was a huge influence in my life; he taught me that if you have passion, you can achieve anything; he never gave up on us as a group. I was awarded the band award for grade nine and my sister, Sandra, was awarded the grade eight award. I ran into him in a bar in Edmonton years later. I bought him a couple of beers, and we reminisced about old times. I mentioned how much of a positive influence he had on my life. Thanks, Mr. Ochoa.

I remember coming home one night and Paul was in bed, crying. We shared the same room, so I asked him what was wrong. He said he fell off his skateboard. Then he showed me his arm; you could see the bone, but it didn't break the skin. I knew it was broken and asked him if he told Dad. He said he did and Dad told him it was only a sprain; I called Dad, and when he came into our room, I told him Paul's arm was broken and showed him. Dad took Paul to the hospital, and he got a cast. Paul was a tough little bastard; I never told him that. He was fearless; he played hockey and couldn't skate but never gave up, and his progress was remarkable. He would fly around and was a good playmaker; he didn't mind laying a body check to guys twice his size. Breaking his arm gave Mom the chance to pull him from hockey before he killed himself.

In 1979, I was going to St. Joseph's High School, doing well in all my classes, and then Mom and Dad decided to move back to Ireland. I quit school and worked at McDonald's 'till we left to go home. This felt kind of weird, as I was established now in Canada; I had lots of friends and a social life. We went back to Ireland where Dad was partnered with this miserable bitch running a meat packing plant. She did have a cute daughter, whom I had a couple of dates with; her name was Angela. Ireland was not for me. I was busting my ass and getting nowhere, but that is the story of my life. Dad and I left to come back to Canada six weeks later; we went to Kitchener, but that didn't work out, so we came back to Edmonton a few days later. Dad told a lie to get a job; one of his buddies built a crate to ship back to Ireland, and Dad bullshitted the guy who shipped it for us, telling him that he built it. He wanted the crate returned to Canada. Dad was now the crate maker for Kuhne and Nagel after seizing the opportunity. Mom, Sandra, and Paul stayed in Ireland until Paul finished the school year.

I went back to St. Joe's to register for the same classes I had before I left, but they were all full, so I said, "Screw it, I'm going to work, then." I went to McDonald's and they hired me on the spot. Within three months, I was a swing manager; then I was transferred to the St. Albert store. This was a big change for me, but I coped. I learned at that age that I liked things to be consistent and predictable with little or no stress. I met the girl I wanted to spend the rest of my life with at that McDonald's; her name was Charlene Muir. She was shy, beautiful, and had a fantastic smile; she was smart and cared about me. Also, she loved people and animals.

I got married for the first time when I was nineteen to a girl I had dated for twelve months before I asked her to marry me; a year and a half later we did. Now Charlene Muir became Charlene O'Riordan. We were newlyweds in June of 1982; she was only eighteen. Charlene was and still is a beautiful person whom I still care a great deal about, as well as her mom, Janette, and dad, Kenneth Muir, whom I had many good times with, but had many battles with, too. Charlene's brother, Roger, was a good friend to me. Roger was mentally handicapped, but I treated him like a brother. I took him out, gave him a job, and enjoyed his company; we both enjoyed wrestling and would go every week. We would go to the bar and watch strippers first and then enjoy our night out watching the fights. Charlene's younger sister, Vicky, was fun to hang out with. I also enjoyed her husband, Greg, when they got married and used to drag him out with Roger on Saturday nights.

I was a father by the time I was twenty-one. Angela was born on November 19, 1983, and I had daughter number two, Deirdre, on February 11, 1986. By the time I was twenty-three, I was married, had two children. I used to get these feelings that something was wrong and bail out for a while; this happened three times. I was divorced by the time I was twenty-seven. It was hell on Charlene; at the time, she was living with a monster. She could do nothing right in my eyes. I was critical of everything. Of course, I would find out later why this was. I filed for bankruptcy during our marriage; we had a lot of hard times, but a lot of good ones, too. Charlene was my first real love. I am sorry that I did not live up to my end of the deal. I thank her husband, Darrel, for picking up the ball with Angela and Deirdre by taking very good care of them. Darrel and I didn't see eye to eye on a lot of situations, but I admired his courage; he has always been good to the girls.

I made up for a lost youth after Charlene and I divorced. I partied hard, slept with lots of women, and frankly, didn't care what I did. I drank like a fish pretty much every night of the week. It was taking its toll on my work; I worked for my dad in the crating business he established called Rimat Crating. Everything else in my life was in shambles now also. I was still in control (or so I thought). I was out with my friend Graham—we share the same birthday—and I asked this lady to dance. She turned me down, then told me to dance with her friend, which I did. I started small talk with the woman I was turned down by; then we started to hit it off. She would now dance with me. After a while, we started kissing on the dance floor; it was fun and intriguing. Her name was Corinne Raiche. I drove her home, made a date with her for midweek, and never looked back.

I got married for the second time at the age of twenty-eight to Corinne Raiche on November 17, 1990, after three months of dating. She was now Corinne O'Riordan. I believed that I had everything figured out. I did not want any more children, as Corinne had a son, Daniel, and I did not want more kids to go through what Angela and Deirdre were going through. Low and behold, I had another daughter a year and a half later; Cassandra was born March 12, 1992. Corinne was a good wife who I just flat out neglected; she did not deserve the treatment she got from me. The other women, the drinking, or the constant worrying I put her through: I was a terrible husband. This marriage was not going well, either; it was very stressful. We fought all the time. I was now running my own crating business in Calgary, Rimat Crating Calgary Ltd. It was going well, very busy but cash poor. I was in constant stress; my only relief was the bar. I spent most nights there; my life was about to change forever. I worked ridiculous hours, couldn't sleep or eat, but boy, could I drink.

It was a cold Friday, January the 7, to be exact; the year was 1995. I had not slept in about four days. I was very irritable. I was owed over twenty thousand dollars from my biggest customer; my mortgage was due; I owed suppliers money. I had a hard time getting a check from this company but I finally got my check. The NHL was also on strike, so no hockey; I was totally stressed out. I was not thinking rationally; then, I told Corinne that I was taking a cab to Edmonton. Remember, I had not slept in four days, my brain was racing, and I could not shut it off. I was not rational; there is no way she could have stopped me, even if she wanted to.

The cab driver stopped in Red Deer to fuel up. He was a nice guy; he was heading to Saskatoon the next day for his father's funeral. We were talking about the hockey strike and CFL football. He was a Saskatchewan Roughrider fan, and then it happened: I told him I had it all figured out. I told him he could own the Roughriders and that I was God. I then asked him to pull the car over, which he did; I left him my wallet with over a thousand dollars in it, as well as some hockey tickets to an old timers' game along with all my credit cards. I started walking back to Calgary. We were near Ponoka. The cab driver was pleading with me to get out of the cold and to get back in the cab. I would have none of it. He took off; I was walking the highway, thinking I was in Ireland. I had Irish music playing in my head. One second I was God; the next, I was the devil. I don't know how far I walked or how long I was out there, but I noticed red and blue lights on the other side of the road. It was the Royal Canadian Mounted Police, along with the cab driver. They could not cross the median as there was too much snow. The officer was turning his siren on and off to get my attention; I crossed the highway, lucky not to have been hit by oncoming traffic.

I was now in the back of the police car; the officer was asking me questions. He stated the cab driver needed to be paid. I told him that my wallet was in the car, that he could have it all, that I didn't need it, and that I was God. He said he would be right back. He went to the cab, paid the driver, then came back, gave me my wallet, and asked if I was okay. Then he started driving. In a few minutes, he walked me into a building. I had no idea where I was. He asked me to sit in a chair while he talked to a lady at reception. The next thing I remember is being in handcuffs and hogtied. I did not know where I was or what was going on; there were cops all around, a female cop with her boot on my neck to keep me down. I was later told that I had slid off the chair and the officer tried to help me up, and I proceeded to assault him. I was in the mental hospital in Ponoka. It would be home for the next thirty days, as I was committed as a danger to others and myself. This was the worst experience of my life; they carried me up to the padded room still in handcuffs and still hogtied. I was then strapped to the bed and asked all kinds of questions. My answer was the same to all: "Go eff yourself." I hate being confined at the best of times, but this was awful. I had to piss in the worst way. I would tell them I had to pee, and they would come in and hold a bucket or whatever it's called for me to pee in. I couldn't do it so, I'd tell them to eff off and spit at them, as I could do nothing else.

They had a nurse stationed outside my room to monitor me, and I scared the shit out of him when I sat up in the bed and rocked it to get out the door. He talked about this the whole time I was there; I wanted to get the hell out of there, but my stay had just begun. It would be the longest and best month, as I had to worry only about me. I would have a shadow for four days; I could do nothing without this person, and I mean nothing. I had now been strapped to the bed for over twelve hours and still needed to take a leak. I told him and he came in with the bucket again. I could not go; for whatever reason, I could not do it. I finally ended up pissing myself. In the twelve hours I was there, I had convinced myself I was God; I had meetings with Gary Betman, the commissioner of the NHL. I had Walter Gretzky and Wayne with me. I told Walter to go kick Betman in the nuts and get this feckin' strike over with. I was somewhat upset there was no hockey. I called Wayne because I knew how he admired his dad as I admired mine, and Wayne was always the same after he had success; it never went to his head. I had meetings with Garth Brooks, told him to keep working hard, and also with world leaders telling them to get their shit together. It was a great feeling. It was better than any drug high; it was peaceful.

Now, at this point, I figured I was Jesus, my father was God, and my father-in-law, Louis Raiche, was the Holy Spirit. I thought I would be resurrected in three days with all my pain gone. Corinne, Sandra, and Paul all came at once to see me. I gave them all orders on what needed to be done. I told Paul it was okay for me to say the eff word, as I was Jesus, and left. Their visit with me lasted all of thirty seconds; I went back to my bed. Of course, that resurrection did not happen after three days. Reality set in. I was one screwed-up puppy. I was diagnosed with bipolar disorder; I had never heard of it. They explained it to me very well. I would have to take medication to be stable for the rest of my life.

I only ever saw my dad cry once in my life, and that was the day I met him in the mental hospital after I had my major breakdown. I arranged a private meeting through my doctor, and we had a quiet room with some furniture and paintings on the wall. Ma and Dad cut their trip to Ireland short to be home for me. Anyway, Dad and I started to talk. I asked him to stand up; I gave him the biggest hug I ever gave anyone. I kissed him on the cheek, told him I loved him; all of this was the first time we ever did this, as our family was not very affectionate. We stood there and bawled like babies, and my dad knew it was my way of telling him I would get better. He visited me a lot and bailed me out of the hospital to go for pizza or coffee.

Corinne was there for me; I broke up with her while I was in the hospital. I cannot begin to imagine how she must have felt; it was not nice, not pretty, but I was sick, and as I said earlier in this book, being sick is not an excuse. I blamed everyone and took it out on everyone.

I read about the illness as much as I could, as I still did not like to read; I asked lots of questions, talked to people in the know. The worst thing about this illness is that you think you are fine and people around you think you're off the wall. The way I like to explain it is if you break your leg, you get a cast; everyone knows you're injured. When you have a mental illness, no one knows. I really don't know what normal is. I think I'm normal; who knows what normal is, anyway? The brain is the most complex part of the body; they have not even touched the surface when it comes to mental illness, what causes it or how to treat it. I live a somewhat normal life; I was lucky that I was able to recover. Some people never get out of the hospital; I now know the warning signs and go get help. It is not easy for the people who live with me, though; you see, I have to watch what I say and do. I find you can be your own worst enemy if you don't think and use common sense. It is workable, though;

I find that doing routine things helps, but as I said earlier, everyone is different.

I have no shame in admitting I have bipolar disorder. Everyone who is close to me knows of my condition. I was released for a weekend pass into the custody of my parents for a visit with my children, Angela and Deirdre. It was almost impossible for me to explain to my daughters what was going on; they were scared, not sure what to expect, and worried for me.

I went back to the hospital Sunday evening, tired, stressed out, as I didn't know if I could face the real world again. For the first time, I, David O'Riordan, was scared to death. I had lots of time to think about my life while I cried for hours that night. I missed Corinne; it's hard to kick someone to the curb when you truly love him or her because you are so scared of yourself. Hospital was boring. I got on the crew to shovel snow just to stay busy. There was group therapy in the afternoon; then we might play floor hockey in the evenings. I was discharged from the hospital on February 1, 1995; then a new life started for me.

I would like to thank all the staff at the Ponoka mental hospital in Ponoka, Alberta, Canada, for your kind gestures and words of encouragement. You all deserve my thanks for the excellent care you provided me; I appreciate your efforts to this day—thanks a million. Also, to Mike, the co-op taxi driver: you saved my life. I will never forget that. To all the RCMP officers: thanks for your help, too. My life had a new beginning now; it would be a challenge to just exist and cope with the hand I was now dealt. I relied on family and friends to enable me to feel normal while accepting the illness that I would have to experience for the rest of my life.

The first thing I had to do was educate myself more about bipolar disorder while adjusting to the daily life of medications. I have never been one to visit the doctor, so this was all new to me, but I learned fast. I was now going to take proper care of myself and ask questions. I also learned that I had two disorders that were incurable, and one would play on the other, so I have always put the brain before the skin, and it has worked pretty well for me.

The one problem I had to deal with was not remembering assaulting the RCMP officer the night I had my breakdown. I had always argued against the legitimacy of people saying they didn't remember killing someone or committing some other act while they were on trial, and now, I can understand that it does happen, but I never believed it before my ordeal. However, that said, I do believe that people should be held accountable for their actions.

Chapter 2

The Realization

I remember the drive home from the hospital: it was almost an hour drive; Dad and I talked, but not about much. Then, with the curiosity of a small child, I asked him if he ever talked to himself. He kind of looked at me; I said, "Yes, I am crazy." "No, you're not; I talk to myself all the time," he said. I had worked with Dad for a pile of years in Edmonton, then started a division of Rimat crating in Calgary with the help of some financial backing from a friend. Also, with a lot of help from Dad, I had the company going pretty well and was wondering how it was doing. We talked about that, too. I stayed at Mom and Dad's for a few weeks.

In the time I was in Edmonton, I met with Corinne; she was at her parents' home in Morinville, just north of Edmonton. She had Danny and Cassie with her. We had a visit; we cried lots; we met a few more times before I asked her if she wanted to give the marriage another try. We agreed to go slowly. She travelled with me to Calgary; we left Danny and Cassie with Corinne's mom and dad. We stopped in Red Deer for a break, where we met Ken and Jeanette Muir, my first wife's parents, going into the Smitty's. They wished me well, as well as all the best, and then gave me a big hug. I had contacted Janette the night I had my breakdown. She worked for the Alberta Union of Provincial Employees, and I thought she might be able to help me get the word out about fixing the hockey strike. Of course, I was out of my mind; she was trying to calm me down, and I just kept going off.

When we arrived in Calgary, I stayed at the house while Corinne stayed with her friend Carol. That was a long night; I didn't sleep, which now scares me when that happens. I listened to music, trying to relax, but couldn't. Corinne arrived at about 9:00 AM; she was worried about my mental state. While talking during the last few weeks, I had decided to put the house up for sale. I thought it would be easier to rent a house in case we changed plans and went back to Edmonton. She called the hospital; they told me to go to my doctor. They referred me to this doctor, so they got me in quickly. I can't remember his name now, but he was taking my personal information; he was typing with his back to me. He was pecking as I do; you can't call it typing. He spoke broken English; then, I had enough. I told him Corinne would give him all the info; I was agitated along with being frustrated with this guy; he sure knew it. I didn't go off on him, but I sure wanted to. I got medication to make me sleep, and I had a good night's sleep. Corinne stayed at the house with me that night.

We hung out for a week or so, looking for a place to live. We found a house to rent where I negotiated with the landlord to redo the basement for cheaper rent. I gutted the basement in a week. I went into work; then, all of a sudden, I knew I wasn't ready for the pressure along with the stress of this again. Even though it was my business, I could not give a shit. I didn't care about it anymore. No amount of alcohol or money could convince me otherwise. I talked to Corinne; we decided to walk now. She would go back to her parents' while I would stay to finish the sale of the house. The landlord was pissed at me, but I did say sorry to him. I took the first offer on the house, making me now free to go back to Edmonton. My financial partner understood; I signed my 40 percent back to him. He assumed all responsibility, as well as liabilities; now, I was done.

I had made arrangements to live with my mom and dad. I was sick and didn't know it; I was now in severe depression. My doctor in Edmonton was Dr. Rowand; she had always taken excellent care of me, so I went and told her my issues. She lined me up with Dr. Edes; I was in to see him within the week. He was a giant of a man, a rugby player–type from South Africa. He was tremendous. I was seeing him every week, and he understood what I was going through. He prescribed the proper medications, lithium and Effexor. He also took into consideration my skin disorder, then had me go to my dermatologist, as it was the worst I had ever had. I had seen Dr. Talpash for years; he put me on Soritane right away. I was back in my comfort zone. I was home in Edmonton with professionals that could help me. I liked Calgary; it is beautiful, but Edmonton is home. I was glad to be back.

I battled depression for months. I stayed off the booze, but life was hard. I was adjusting to a new way of life. I went out on the weekends to a country nightclub called The Rattlesnake Saloon; as I've told you, I always enjoyed music. The Snake had live bands; they were top of the circuit. I only drank Coke while mingling with the crowd. I was getting my confidence back, plus starting to feel better about my life and myself. I had been living with Mom and Dad for six months; now, money was short; my long-term disability insurance didn't kick in yet. I was getting behind on payments; my child support was in arrears, and I needed to do something about it. Corinne helped me with a résumé; she did an excellent job for me.

I was able to get a couple of weeks' work from an old boss of mine at West Edmonton Mall. Kevin Hanson was his name. I had worked for the mall years ago, starting as a clean-up person after tradesmen, which was only a summer position that turned into a two-year gig for me. Kevin was the electrical coordinator. He invited me to work on his crew as the light man. The couple of weeks were spent painting in fantasy land and got me in contact with old friends I had worked with and had me feeling good about myself again.

Dad was happy for me; he encouraged me on. Mom was positive, too. I still went to see Dr. Edes every couple of weeks. He was happy that I was making progress. I still went to The Snake on the weekends; I would now have a couple of beers. I had made some friends and was sitting with them when this guy asked me if the lady sitting next to me was my wife or girlfriend. I said, "No, that's my friend Susan; have at her; get her up dancing." This fellow's name was Tim Johnson. We became fast friends; he and Susan dated for a while, but it didn't last. Tim has remained my friend for all these years. I'll tell you more about him later.

I would pick up my children, Angela and Deirdre, and take them out a couple of times a week to visit with them. They were getting big, and I always enjoyed spending time with them. It was hard to deal with the fact that I didn't see the kids a lot, an hour or two a couple of times a week. I saw Corinne and the kids a couple of times a week as well; I always enjoyed our time with each other.

It was hard for me to accept that I had broken up two families with this illness, ruined people's hopes or dreams, and above all, screwed up my own life. I was ashamed of my life and myself and just wanted it over with, but I did not want my children to deal with their dad killing himself. I am a proud man; I believe in Jesus, so I stuck it out. I was driving my parents crazy; they had a hard time coping with my lifestyle. I was up all night, slept all day; my dad was really getting pissed off. No one knew the pain I was going through. I just wanted to give up, saying, "That's it." I had several plans to kill myself, all elaborate, to look like accidents so my kids could get the insurance money.

I kept my faith in God, tried as best as I could. I started flogging out résumés again; then, as I was driving by a company I used to do a lot of crating for, I decided to drop in and say hi. It's funny how things work in life, because by the end of the day, Dennis Crouteau offered me a job at Griffith Oil Tool. It was an easy transition for me, as I knew a lot of the people working there already, and the work was familiar. I started the next day. Dad was delighted, as was I, as I embarked on a new adventure. I hit it off with the fellows and enjoyed what I was doing.

With bipolar disorder new to me, it had been about nine months since my breakdown. I had to keep my guard up, be careful of what I said and did. I doubted myself a lot then, started drinking again, fairly hard, about five nights a week, with the boys from work. My friend Tim and I were hanging out a lot more now, too. Tim was a short, stocky guy at about five feet, five inches. We used to talk, laugh, drink, and fight while chasing the ladies, and we were a pretty good combination who enjoyed having fun while listening to the bands. Tim understood me; we connected; we were both broke, both in dire straits, but could always laugh about our situations. We were never short of stories, and we enjoyed each other's company. We were both big dreamers with great ideas, just too much baggage to make things happen—also, of course, no money to do it, either.

It was the night before New Year's Eve, and I went for a few beers at The Snake. I left the bar at 2:00 AM and headed home. I was driving up the alley when the flashing lights went on, and I stopped right away. The officer informed me they were doing a random check stop. "Did you have anything to drink?" I told him I had had five beers between 8:00 and 1:00. I blew the roadside test and failed. They parked my car at home, and then took me to the breathalyser bus, where I failed again. I was now arrested for impaired driving.

Being the guy I am, I told my parents the next morning; my dad was upset but dealt with the news better than I thought he would. Mom was pissed off. "Everything happens to you," she said. It was just another challenge to face. I would plead not guilty on the advice of my lawyer, Ernie Reed, who was another character. Work was going well; I had a few dollars in the bank. I decided to get my own apartment close to work, in case I did lose my licence. I was happy to have my own place again. Mom and Dad were great, but I needed to move on with my life. The apartment was my home, and I enjoyed it, had friends over. Tim and I would have great laughs; we'd get primed to go to The Snake for a night out. We were the life of the bar; everyone knew us, and we always had fun. Tim was a little shy, so I would get going on the girls and invite them to hang out with us. Tim was in his element then, as he's very funny, so it was my task to get the girls and his task to keep them there. We were a great tag team, always had fun, met lots of wonderful people, and got lucky quite a bit, too.

Tim and I would be out on a Friday night; then, the guys from Griffith would come to the bar, and they would just shake their heads at me. They couldn't believe I was the same guy from work all spruced up while having a good time. Like I said, we owned that bar; we knew every waitress, bartender, as well as all the bouncers. Now, the boys from Griffith liked to drink, but they also liked to fight, as did Tim and I. We found ourselves involved in a few tussles where the cops showed up. Always good for a laugh—I remember one in particular. Tim's brother-in-law, Kelly, was in town; the three of us went to The Snake. It was the weekend, so it was busy. Kelly got pretty drunk; this fellow took exception to something he said or did to his sister; now, the war was on. I remember this because it was so funny: this guy was about six feet, eight or nine inches; Kelly is about six feet, three inches; then, there's Tim, all five feet, five inches of him, in between these two, as I'm just standing back, laughing. Tim asked me for a hand. I told him he was doing just fine. I wish I would have had a video camera, because it would have won the hundred grand on America's funniest home videos.

I went to court in May to fight my impaired charge. I was lucky; the judge understood my frustration as the prosecutor kept badgering me with the same questions. I got a little pissed off at her line of questioning, and the judge finally told her to move on. I was acquitted of all charges, and my lawyer was $5,000 richer.

Corinne and I started working things out again; soon, we were living together as a family. Only this time, I hoped we could make it work; it went well for a couple of years, then became stale. I was drinking lots while not coming home 'till late, but I was doing the family thing. It was Christmas of 1998; we had Mom and Dad over for Christmas dinner. We all shared a few laughs; it was the best Christmas I had had in years. I was unemployed, as I had gotten into a pissing contest with my supervisor and got laid off in October. Now, I was looking for work again; I let my guard down, and I was gone.

I took my stepson, Daniel, to an Edmonton Brickmen indoor soccer game on January 16, 1999, and heard my name announced over the public address system. It didn't sound like me; I heard it a couple more times, then decided to see if it was me. I was informed by my brother, Paul, who was on hold on the phone, that Dad had died of a massive heart attack. For sure, that was the saddest day in my life; there is not a day that goes by when I don't think about you, Dad. You were my hero, and if I can be half the man you were, I'll be doing well. By the way, look up Mr. Sullivan and Brother Sommers and drop a couple of your famous rousers on them; you know, the ones that would knock a buzzard off a shit wagon and make them gag for days.

Thanks, Dad, for everything you ever did for me. I understand your teaching and appreciate the life that you have shown me. You have inspired me by making each day bearable just in thinking of you and talking to you. Also, Dad, you were a pretty good-looking son of a bitch, as I now see you in the mirror every day—no comb over, though you look better bald. It's funny for me now to have said "Yeah, yeah, and yea" all those years and now to replay all of those conversations while truly understanding how you were trying to make me a man who could be proud of his family and also his life.

Of course, you were not always right; of course, I wasn't always wrong, but the day you died, Dad, I did become a man. I live in your shoes, and by the way, thanks for the couple of suits; they look good on me, but I didn't need them that badly or that soon. You taught me compassion, honesty, integrity, and above all, to love your family. I have kind of screwed that up, but that can always change, though. After my dad's death, I had it rough for a couple of days and had Corinne take me to the hospital, as I couldn't sleep and felt the warning signs of a breakdown. The psychiatrist on call knew what I was going through and got me sorted out, which was a good thing, as three of Dad's brothers were to arrive the following night from Ireland. I was in good shape when I met them and visited at Mom and Dad's house.

Dad's brothers—Michael, and his wife, Jenny; Donal, and his wife, Terry; and Liam, and his daughter, Dawn—all made the trip from Ireland for the funeral. It was nice to see them all and have a few laughs about the past. Michael and Jenny were here before on a holiday, so it was new for Donal and Liam, and they were disappointed that they had never made the trip before, when Dad was alive. Everyone was admiring Dad's bar, as well as how well it was stocked; he had bottles from every country, with collector's bottles; it was his hobby. The funeral was on Saturday. All I wanted was to keep it together until that was over; I stayed off the booze and took the relations out to see some of Edmonton. It was cold that week, very cold, and they were not used to it, but they did enjoy themselves.

Friday night was the prayer service, and the chapel was full. Its' amazing how many people you know but don't realize you know them. The Irish club was well represented; Dad was playing cards with the lads in the Don club right before he died. Saturday was now upon us, and I was not looking forward to it. We were in a room at the back of the church, and my nephew, Matt, started acting up. He was only about eight, and I took him out, gave him shit, and told him to respect Granddad. He did not act up again. I felt bad for getting so pissed off at him. Paul and I draped the casket with the Irish flag at the start of the service. I held it together until the eulogy, when Paul's friend Rob did the speech; he did an excellent job.

The funeral was now over; we went to the funeral home to say our last goodbyes to Dad. I thanked Matt later on that day and told him I was proud of his actions and for his appropriate behavior during the funeral;

he was glad to see I was not upset at him anymore. We said goodbye to the relations on Wednesday, and then, our loss as a family really set in. Life would never be the same, especially for Mom. There were lots of decisions to make. I was glad not to be working, but I was not doing Mom any favors, as I would argue about everything. It was hard for all of us to cope with everything.

I started a new position with Cascade Geotechnical in March of 1999 as shipper/yard foreman. Now I was back on track, career-wise. I enjoyed the challenge very much; also, the owners were very good to me. Craig Miller, Gordon Dennis, and Bruce Miller: thanks for the opportunity. I enjoyed working with your companies. My duties were to handle the day-to-day shipping and receiving aspects of Cascade's diverse group of companies. Craig and Bruce were brothers who had started a fencing company and built it into a fabulous business, doing contracts for all the major house builders and subdivisions. Craig is worth a good chunk of change now, but he has never forgotten where he came from. I enjoyed Craig's sense of humor and his attitude, with a small dose of temper thrown into the mix, just to keep me on my toes. Really, I admired him as he had accomplished so much, and he definitely inspired me to believe that the ordinary working person could succeed if he or she made the right sacrifices and commitments to him- or herself. Gordon knew both Craig and Bruce for a lot of years. I would be lying if I said any more than that. I can tell you without hesitation that Gordon is one of the most honest and dedicated people I have ever had the pleasure of knowing. His love of his family is the most genuine and the core of his being.

Gordon managed Cascade Geotechnical and was a partner to Craig in this endeavour. The business consisted of erosion control products, plastic fencing, T-posts, bamboo poles, geotextiles, silt fences, and any other thing we could dream up. Mostly distribution and some in-house manufacturing of inventive products like Enviroberm, sewing, and cutting were all regular operations. Gordon admitted to me shortly after I was hired that he had made a big mistake. I was not Gordon's first choice for the position; he phoned me three weeks after I had interviewed for the position and asked me if I was still looking for work. I was, and he admitted, when I interviewed, that the person he had hired had not worked out. I was delighted to have a job. I didn't care that I was second choice, but Gordon told me a couple of weeks into the job that the only reason I was second choice the first time was because the other fellow would work for less money than me. Gordon was funny and honest at the same time.

Ken Heroun was a crew foreman for Cascade fencing that I thought was a prick. He would get on his guys and never let up; we had a few war of words; then, I realized Ken was very passionate about his work. He just had a different way of showing it, while I had a different way of viewing it. I started looking at it from his point of view and working with him instead of against him. We had mutual respect for each other and developed into good working buddies and shared lots of time brainstorming. Ken was a positive influence and fun to know; he had passion to burn as far as work goes. He is a genuine, hardworking man that loves to shoot pool. Russell Kelly was another crew foreman; he was different in the way he approached things, and I worked with him, too. How people react to you is all in how you treat people. I am good at reading people and what they are about. I enjoy a hard day's work and going for a beer after to talk about it, and I did this lots with Russell. Work has always been my passion and a sense of self worth and a feeling of pride, With the family at Cascade changing so much as staff turned over, there were key people that you got to know and considered family.

Gilbert Barber was one of those people. Gil was a pleasure to work with; he was older, like a father figure. We had lots of ideas, lots of laughs, and a few disagreements, with great stories of how he did this and that. He was a definite sales manager, and we nicknamed him "The Professor." Leslie Copeland was the bravest woman I know for working with all of us wild and crazy guys. She was the office manager and gained the respect of all employees. Leslie is very loyal and as honest as they come; she was a sounding board for me lots of times with personal issues and a genuine friend. We worked closely together, and I learned a lot about the character of a person from Leslie. Her family was very important, and the love she had for her grandson Austin was inspiring; she also was a very talented artist who did beautiful needlepoint. I had the pleasure of seeing her creations, and frankly, I was blown away with her talent and precise attention to detail.

Last but not least is Bruce Miller; I saved Bruce for last out of respect for myself. There are all kinds of things in life that people regret not doing, like keeping up with old friends or going to the concert, maybe getting that dog, and so on. My best description of Bruce is this: unpredictable, sometimes annoying, funny, and he has a lot of great qualities and some bad ones, also. I am a workingman with a great respect for the chain of command. That said, I deal with an illness that is unpredictable, and to me, sometimes, unwanted. Bruce was my reason for leaving Cascade, and you will read more about that later. My regret now that I look back is that I never went and talked to Craig or Gordon after the fact with a cooler head and a different attitude. Bruce, I will say this: I apologize for what happened. I loved my family at Cascade and took great pride in working for an excellent organization. I made a mistake letting bipolar disorder get the better of me on that day, and I have regretted that for many years. I also have regretted not talking to you since I left. Bipolar disorder is bad, but being stubborn is foolish. Thanks to all at Cascade for some great memories.

Another aspect of bipolar disorder is promiscuity; I was out with Tim one Friday night when I hit it off with a lady in the bar. We were kissing and carrying on. She wanted me to go back to her place, but I was with Corinne. Later that night, while having cheese toast at Boston Pizza, I told Tim that I had to end it with Corinne, as that was no way to have a relationship. He helped me move the following weekend, and Corinne and I were now done for good.

I then became a pig and slept with any woman I could; I am not proud of that, but I did it. Women were toys to me, so I played with them when they would let me. I still had class, but I know I hurt some people along the way. Realizing as well as accepting that I have bipolar disorder did change my life in those five years—some for the good and a lot for the bad, too.

Life will never be as it was; that's for certain, but you must carry on and have meaning in your existence. Bipolar disorder is an illness that will kick your ass if you let it; it is day to day with different results for everyone. You must stay focused on every aspect of your life to succeed. Getting proper sleep and a decent diet with exercise is a good start. Also, never be afraid to ask for help; the mental health professionals are very good at understanding what you are going through. Tim was a big support for me at this time; we would talk and laugh for hours. We understood each other and that helped us cope with life's challenges on a daily basis. Tim enjoyed his scotch, so when we were dividing up Dad's bottles from the bar, I put dibs on a few bottles, and I gave them to him.

Dad had a story about a bottle of Ballantine's scotch that he only ever shared with me. It was a bottle that he obtained in, let's say, a not so honourable fashion. He was in the hospital for blood clots; he was there for about two weeks and decided to go AWOL one Saturday afternoon. He went to the warehouse we sublet from another company. The fellow that owned that company, Peter Perkins, had a private bar in his office. He was going to open this particular bottle fairly soon. Dad swiped the bottle and could never be blamed for it, as he was in the hospital. This happened in the mid-eighties, and he could never tell anyone until he told me around 1995. Tim and I toasted Dad every Friday for a few weeks, taking care to savor the taste and appreciate the way good scotch is really to be enjoyed.

I met my third wife on a Saturday night, March 12, 2000, to be exact. I was at The Snake with Tim. The Prairie Dogs were playing. We had met Tim and Sheila a few months back and enjoyed their music; they were a great band. They knew we were out for a laugh and would banter with us and join us on their breaks. It was about 1:30 in the morning and this lady asked me to dance. Thinking nothing of it, I said sure; she told me her name was Melanie. We danced; then, the band started playing "Momma Let Him Play," so I told her I had to go and sing, then left her on the dance floor. I jumped on stage, did the song, which I did with the Prairie Dogs all the time. I always sang that song with them and always had fun doing it. It's a rush to get up on stage and feel like a rock star. When I came off the stage, Melanie came and told me I was great, and we danced again. Tim and I went back to Melanie's place with her friends; we had a couple of pizzas after the bar closed. We stayed for a couple of hours; then, I kissed her goodnight; then, she gave me her phone number. I called her on the Sunday and talked to her for hours; I was to check her out at her bowling next Wednesday. One thing lead to another, and I spent the night there. I moved in with her and her son, Evan, a short time later. I filed for bankruptcy again, as I had Revenue Canada on my back for taxes, which I didn't believe I owed. After two and a half years of fighting, I gave up.

Melanie was seven years older than me; we were married December 11, 2000, but it did matter after a couple of years. She was excellent the first two years, but then, she did everything she could to change me. Between the stress of home and the job, I lost it one day at work when Bruce was giving me grief about some menial bullshit. He was yelling at me, and I lost it on him. To be honest, I wanted to beat the shit out of him, and I had a rage going through me and there and then, I quit my job. It was a stupid decision, but I know it was the right one, because I left with my head held high and not in handcuffs. I would have put a serious beating on Bruce, and I know that's not right. So now, my career with Cascade was over, and I was looking for work again; it seems to be my bipolar shoes.

A couple of weeks later, I got a job through Kelly Services working for Ashland Chemical as a material handler. Kevin Shopik, the plant manager for Ashland Edmonton, hired me on full time six months later. There were six of us working in the plant; it was a comfortable environment for me. I enjoyed my job; also, the people I worked with were diverse and funny. David Balon, John Bontron, Chris Lennox, and Marko Viera, along with Kevin and me as the new man made the team of six for operations. We worked well as a team and worked hard to build the business. The job involved working with, near, and around dangerous chemicals, which I had no problem performing; there were a few minor spills that we were trained to handle. It is not an environment that everyone could feel comfortable working in, but I did, and again, I was learning and enjoying it. This was the best job I had since working for myself: good pay, great benefits, and freedom to suggest ways of making the operations of the plant more efficient.

My marriage was also back on track, now that I was working. It wasn't great, but it was working. Angela was now living with me; she was in her final year of high school and working at Zellers Restaurant part time. She also has the rare skin disease, Darier's, that I have, which I had a hard time coping with because I knew what she was going through. Angela, however, understood that it wasn't my fault and accepted the cards that life had dealt her. She is very special to me, and I have learned a lot from her ways of thinking and her positive outlook on life. It was fun to have her back in my life every day, but we did have our battles. I pushed her to be the best that she could be, and I wasn't always right to do that. In May of 2004, Angela rented the basement of Mom's house; she was now independent, or so she thought. She was only out of the house a few days when I was moving in with Mom also.

I have no children with Melanie, so I haven't seen her or her son, Evan, since she decided we weren't meant to be and kicked my ass out in May of 2004. I was working ten to twelve hours a day; she was working six hours, at most, and she wanted me to cook and clean even though she took Fridays off. I had issues with that and told her to fly a kite. Then, I bought a car she didn't want me to buy and told me I wouldn't get financing. She didn't like it when I came home with the car the next day. I didn't have a relationship with Tim for five years because he disliked her; now, we are best buddies again. My biggest problem with Melanie is she knew I was bipolar before we ever got together, then did nothing to educate herself about it. I spent a few months with Mom and Angela; I then got my own apartment so I was independent again.

I started a new chapter in my life in 2004. I traveled to Ireland with my sister, Sandra; it had been eighteen years since I was home. It was long overdue, and it was a wonderful trip. I was amazed that things had not changed a whole lot. The people were great, nice, and friendly; it was very familiar to me. It was great to see everyone again— uncles, aunts, cousins—we had a lot of fun. The highlight of my trip was a visit we made to the Arin Islands, which had spectacular scenery: the cliffs were awesome, the views breathtaking. I sat on the edge of a cliff and thought how great life is. I thought about my kids, all the good things in my life; then, I washed all the misfortune away. I felt great, a new me.

When I got back from Ireland, everything was good for a while; then, I went into a state of depression again. It was the worst I had ever had. I told my boss, Kevin, everything that was going on with me, including being bipolar, and he was very accommodating, putting me in the satellite warehouse for a few months; it was a lot less stressful. It took me about six months to shake the depression with the help of doctors and medication. I have surrounded myself with new friends who are very positive and have been very good for me.

In December of 2004, I was out with friends from work, celebrating one of their birthdays with the Christmas season. I left the club at 12:30 AM to go home, and then was pulled over at a check stop. Now I was arrested with my second impaired driving charge. I was extremely agitated but did not portray this to the officer. I could not believe this, as I had not drank that much: three pints, to be exact. I called my lawyer, but he was now retired, so he gave me another number to call the next day. I was returned to the nightclub by the officer, and then got a ride home with my friends. I called the lawyer whose name was Mr. Fix; we arranged an appointment. It was a new practice in Edmonton that you had three weeks to get your affairs in order, and then, you would surrender your licence for three months, regardless of being innocent or guilty. I walked for the three months and had my friend Marlene drive me wherever I needed to go with my car. She would pick me up every morning and take me to work, then pick me up in the afternoon to take me home. It was inconvenient but a good learning lesson. I got my licence back on the twenty-seventh of March 2005.

Edmonton is a beautiful city, but it is hard to get around when you don't drive. Then, throw the winter in on top of that, with minus thirty temperatures, snow, and wind; it makes it really hard. I got through it all and had a new appreciation for the privilege of driving and the freedom that a car provides. Also, I knew how lucky I was to have a friend like Marlene; she was terrific in her understanding and willingness to help me out. I met Marlene on a Web site called Canadian Personals in 2004; we became good friends and had a lot in common and did a lot of things together. I enjoyed her company as we always laughed, and she somewhat understood my moods and outlook on life. I had met people from all over Canada on this Web site and enjoyed chatting with everyone. I met Christine from PEI and went to visit her in April of 2005; that was a great trip. I saw the whole island and the history of confederation. Christine was not my type of woman, but we did enjoy our visit together and talked for hours. I rented a keyboard and gave her a concert. It was a wonderful experience visiting Christine and seeing all of PEI; it was a long trip, but it was worth it.

In early May, I met another woman online. Her name is Heather Morrow; she has four boys, aged eleven, eight, and twins that were six at the time we met. We arranged to meet on the long May weekend in Saskatoon, as the boys were going to their dad's for a visit. It was awkward at first with Heather, as we had only talked on the phone and didn't know what to expect from each other. I was excited, as I knew she was what I was looking for in a relationship; she had the same background as me, with her parents being from Scotland. We shared a lot of the same traditions and customs and an ability to read each other very well right off the hop. We had a few fumbling moments right out of the block, but the weekend was superb, with every chance of becoming a permanent relationship. I was scheduled to go to court at the end of May for the impaired charge, so I wanted to meet her before that, as I didn't know how court was going to turn out.

May 27, 2005, was court day. I picked Tim up to come for moral support and to drive my car home in case I lost. I was a nervous wreck, and he calmed me down with his jokes and kidding around. I had met my lawyer the day before, and he took me through a mock trial to give me a chance to experience what the prosecution would ask and get me familiar with the procedures. He told me not to engage in conversation with anyone. The trial started, and there was no evidence except the notes of the arresting officer presented against me. I took the stand and answered every question put to me without being nervous; in fact, I was excellent, which was surprising, as I'm always petrified in those situations. The expert witness for me was Dr. Malechey; he testified about a test that he put me through involving taking a drink of his concoction and measuring it with time and the breathalyser to come up with accurate readings. After his testimony, I was acquitted of all charges and free to drive. Mr. Fix was now up $7,000, and I would make a commitment to myself of zero tolerance in regards to drinking and driving.

Chapter 3

Daddy's Girls

I have hurt each and every one of my children and stepchildren in one form or another; for that, I am truly sorry. I would say that Angela got the worst of it, with Deirdre a close second. I have no idea what effect the experience of divorce has on children; Cassandra has been on board for that roller coaster as well. I always wanted to be surrounded by beautiful women; I just never expected it to be my wife, ex-wives, and daughters. I am very glad that two of my three daughters are still in my life, even though I have moved away from Edmonton. Deirdre and her partner, Curtis, presented me with a grandson in October of 2006. I stayed with Deirdre, along with the new man, Jacob, for a few days. I hadn't changed diapers in years, certainly not for a boy, so I did have a few firsts.

It is amazing how a baby can make you feel; Jacob was smiley and a joy to hold. It was the first quality time that Deirdre had spent with me, only us, together, in years. We talked about the past; I was able to answer most of her questions. I am very proud of all three of my daughters, each one for different reasons. I would like to take the time to tell you about them, as they are my reason for still being on this planet. As with everything else in this world, time marches on; so do my daughters. They are not children anymore; they are beautiful women now.

Angela has just turned twenty-four; that's hard to believe. She is now cohabitating with a bloke named Alex Laney; she says everything is good. I remember the day Angela was born as if it were only yesterday. She was beautiful; she changed the way I felt about the world immediately. I was not prepared to be a father at such a young age, then all of a sudden, her mother and I had this gorgeous little creature depending on us for survival.

As Angela grew up, she never asked for much, but one Christmas, she did ask for a kitchen set like the one at the daycare; you know, the stove, fridge, and sink—Fisher Price stuff. But Charlene and I could not find it anywhere, so I decided to make a set for her. She was thrilled because these were better than the daycare's, as her daddy made them just for her; on Christmas day, she had to show and tell everyone. Angela has always loved Christmas.

Angela was always very loyal to me, no matter what was going on throughout her life. She was a remarkable child in the way she was to her family, especially Grandma and Nan. She always liked to visit her grandparents on both sides. Early on in her school life, she was devastated because she failed grade one because of the divorce. That was hard for her; however, she did come through it. I can only imagine her strength to be able to deal with our hereditary skin disorder in the manner in which she has done throughout her life. I have an extra special bond with Angela because of Darier's disease for sure, but also I feel she got a rough ride through life as a youngster not knowing where she belonged. Of course, I always wanted to protect her because I felt she was vulnerable and could easily be led in the wrong direction. Angela carried a lot of innocence into adulthood, so I was always afraid she would get burned. While she was living with my mom, I got a call from Mom that Angela was up to no good, that her place was a mess, and that she was having people over—all things that are perfectly fine in my book. After all, she was nineteen years old and paying her rent.

Now, after several of these phone calls from Mom, I found myself between a rock and a hard place. I thought it through as much as anyone really can; I decided that Angela moving out of Mom's house was the best thing to be done. Now Angela is, as I said, very loyal, so I knew there was absolutely no way that I could convince her to move out. So, what the hell was I going to do? I asked myself. I went over to Mom's and Angela's. I talked to Mom, got the low down from her, then said to myself, "This is not fair to Angela; I have to get her out now." She needed her own life while not having her Nan be so intrusive on her space, as well as everything she does.

How the hell was I going to pull this off? How could I do this with the least amount of fallout? Well, I could achieve peace in the family only one way. That was starting a fight with Angela and kicking her out of Mom's house, so that's what I did. I really felt horrible as Angela battled with me; really, it was none of my business to get involved. Sometimes you have to do weird things to make someone see the light by protecting them. This is what I believed I was doing with my child in this case. I have big shoulders that carried the blame and hurt for devastating my daughter but knew in my heart this was in her best interest. Angela and I met a few times; there was lots of tension; then, about six months later, she met me for a pint in Sherlock Holmes Pub, where she told me that what I did was the best thing that had ever happened to her. She really found her independence, and she still had a relationship with her Nan. We exchanged a hug, then started a new relationship as father and grown daughter. I have advised Angela since then; however, she makes her own decisions now; that's the way it should be. She keeps in touch with me; we still talk at least once a week.

Angela has always been an inspiration to me; I have never met someone so loyal, as well as trusting of people, or with such a genuinely good nature towards people. Her family does come first and foremost; she still keeps in contact with my ex-wife Melanie. The thing that impresses me the most about Angela is that she works hard, plays hard, while never giving up on her dreams. I love Angela with all my heart. I'm very proud that she is my daughter.

Angela, please, stay away from the singing, because if I laugh like that anymore, I will die. It was Christmas time when the whole family got together for our gift exchange. Deirdre brought her karaoke machine for everyone to see and listen to. When all the gang had left, there was only Angela, Deirdre, Cassandra, Evan, and Melanie, along with me. Now, I can't remember what song Angela tried to sing, but it was bad. The hand gestures plus energy she was putting into this song were priceless, but she couldn't sing to save her soul. All of us were laughing; then, I took it one step further, becoming inconsolable. Honestly, I haven't laughed like that in years. I excused myself. I went to the bedroom and really started laughing; about fifteen minutes later, I came out with sore sides and with a pain in my belly from laughing so much. All I had to do was look at Angela and I'd start again; it was one of the funniest things I have seen.

Deirdre (pronounced Deardra) is my middle daughter, aged twenty-one; she is the son that every father would die for. A natural athlete who has excelled at many sports, she has tremendous leadership abilities that have paved the way for Deirdre to succeed in life. As a father, I was always impressed with her because she would stick up for her big sister in school. She was never afraid to give one in the snot box to some kid if the need arose, which it did on several occasions. She was tough as nails, while being funny, too; she did pick up a few bad words from me as she grew up that she still uses today. Now, as a new mom, Deirdre is excelling in that role; I am very proud of the job she and Curtis are doing with Jacob. "Grandchild number two arrived, in June 2008"

Deirdre was looking for a job. She liked the pub I went to regularly, then said she would like to work there. She had no experience working in a bar, but I knew she would do well because of her temperament. Deirdre is a lot like me in a lot of ways: she won't take crap from anyone, she is straight out with things, and she is also funny. I talked to the manager at Sherlock's when I was in there, and then told her about Deirdre in passing conversation. This was the first time I ever had to do a sales job for one of my children; I was able to convince Susan to give her an interview. Deirdre met me at the pub the next day, looking professional and eager to meet the challenge; it was busy at the time. Susan was by herself, so Deirdre waited with me. She did introduce herself to Susan, then started chatting with people around the bar. Then, there was a regular named Greg who was in a wheelchair. He was leaving; Deirdre helped him out the door.

Susan had made her decision regarding Deirdre before she ever had the interview that she was going to give this kid a try. That's what she told me later when she talked to me, so Deirdre had the job. It felt good as a dad to be able to get her foot in the door, then watch her take off as one of the best servers in the pub. Deirdre was always good at being coached; I did tell her some expectations people had, what they liked or didn't, but the biggest trait Deirdre has is common sense, and she knows how to read people well. She still works at Sherlock's, only one day a week now; she still enjoys the people.

When I visited Deirdre, I stayed with her and Jacob for those few days. One question she did ask me was why I favored Angela and Cassandra over her when she was younger. My answer to her was simple; I never had to worry about her, as she was always strong and she could take care of herself. Her question did make me feel as though I was wrong to do that to her. We talked, laughed, and cried over those few hours with our bond getting stronger. I now had started the father–grown daughter relationship with Deirdre.

I am very proud of Deirdre; she has accomplished a lot in her young life, even though her childhood was hard. I know there are still issues she needs to deal with. She has come away with the strength along with the determination to succeed at whatever she chooses to do with her life. As critical as I am, I really enjoy listening to Deirdre sing; she has a beautiful voice with a great stage presence that just blows me away. She will ask me what I thought of a song; then, I will give her my honest opinion. Deirdre does know how to sing; she has fun doing it whenever the opportunity presents itself. As children, Angela and Deirdre fought like a cat and a dog. I really thought they were going to kill each other for a few years in their teens. They are best friends now and do whatever they can to help each other out. I have learned a lot from both of them, and I am privileged to be their father.

In all my years of being a father, my kids have always been the most important factor in my life; they have been my strength, my hope, along with my inspiration. There has not been a day that went by when I didn't think about all three of them or wonder how they were doing. It was hard on my children to be products of divorce, and it was also hard on their moms and me. You can choose your friends, but you can't choose your family. Life is structured on survival of the fittest, by how much money you have—no money, no funny. All I ever wanted was for my children to have a better shot than I had.

My third daughter is Cassandra, who is fifteen years old. She lives with my ex-wife Corinne and her brother, Daniel. Cassie, as I like to call her, is not in my life at present by her choice. I have not seen or talked to Cassie in almost two years and would tell her the following saying that I found in my counsellor's office. It goes like this:

Life will always have its share of difficulties—and in the midst of them, YOU can CHOOSE to be a fulfilled, caring, loving, healthy, and balanced person.

Learn to choose happiness in this moment in spite of your circumstances. Instead of concentrating on why you can't be happy, focus your attention on all that is good.

- Identify, release and change how you respond to the past.

- Overcome and let go of your "victim" stance.
- Trade bitterness and resentment for peace and joy.
- Set goals for the future with passion and purpose.

Cut loose the baggage of long ago …

Cassandra has always been very special to me; The day that she was born, however, was very special; I was older now, so delighted to be a dad again. Cassie was very easygoing as a child. She loved to draw, but most of all, she loved to spend time with me. I remember being between jobs, so I walked her to and from school every day; she liked that. Also, the day I went to read at story time in her classroom with all her classmates, she was so proud of her dad.

Cassandra is an excellent artist, as well as Daniel and Corinne. She can draw anything effortlessly. When she was young, I used to get her to draw me the Simpsons characters. She could bang them off in no time. Fairly soon, before she stopped seeing me, I had asked Cassie to draw me a lighthouse on a decent piece of paper. She did this amazing job with charcoal that I loved. Now, it didn't look all that great just on the piece of paper, but I spent a couple hundred dollars and got it framed, so now, it is a work of art in my living room.

Cassie did get her love of music from me; she plays saxophone and is really quite good. She also plays piano and guitar, as well as sings. She is up on all the groups with new songs; she performs with her school band quite regularly.

Life can throw you a curve while you're waiting for a fastball, but you can rest assured life won't walk you. Yes, no free passes here—this is the game of life that we are all playing, whether we like it or not. Just think about it here for a minute: how many dads take their kids to a ball or hockey game in a year? Life is full of metaphors. I am from a generation of misfits who have made a lot of our children suffer because of our mistakes, while we have not tried to improve their circumstances. There are far too many children being raised by one parent while the divorced parents can no longer communicate effectively with the best interests of the child or children at heart. Children are torn between their moms and dads; they love both parents; they didn't want this. I wonder how this will affect their mental health. Of course, there is always the money issue, as well as other problems. I know; I have three daughters from two marriages, so I will never truly know their pain, as I never went through the ordeal of divorce as a child.

Really, I can't imagine what children must go through being torn apart by the two people they admire the most. I do know that it was not easy for my children. Cassie is fifteen; she can make her own decisions to a point. She does know that when she's ready, I will be here for her; after all, I am her dad. Cassie, I can't tell you I know what you're going through I don't. Life can be downright cruel, but it is also what you make of it. Don't spend too much time worrying about the bad things; try to focus on the good and on what you like. I have worked hard all my life, got up in the morning, put on my game face (even though I could hardly think), and then prayed that I could make it through another day of faking it. Yes, it was hard, but I have to pay the bills. The mistake that I made was after work, I would take my game face off; and then, I would take my frustrations out on the people I loved the most. I had no right to do that; however, that's all I knew to keep my sanity. People can change, and I'm proof of that. I don't hide behind the game face anymore; I accept who I am for what I am, and I know that I am a nice person. I do miss you, Cassie; we have a lot of catching up to do. I wrote the poem "Bipolar Shoes" for you. I think and pray for you every day. You are always in my heart.

As a dad, I have made the best effort that I knew to make things work in my relationships with the girls; however, I also know that I made a whole lot of mistakes along the way. Sometimes, I think back while I replay some of the issues that my children had to live through, and I just cringe. My way of expressing my thoughts and feelings doesn't always come across as the way I mean it. I blamed myself for a lot of their hardships and do take responsibility for my actions. I will not, however, beat myself up over things that happened in the past, as they are over now; they are only there when I bring them up. At one point or another, every person in life struggles. So, I feel that how people react to these struggles is a sign of their character. Each one of my children is strong because of the values that their mothers and I instilled in them. They were provided with the tools to cope with life, to survive—yes, they had it hard, but there is always someone who has it harder than you.

Angela, Deirdre, and Cassandra, being the children of a person with a mental illness, you don't know the whole story; you really don't know much about mental illness, either; that is why I decided to write this book. I wanted to give you an opportunity, along with many other people, to learn what bipolar disorder can do to families, so if this book makes one person think, "I do that," or "I have a problem," then I have done my job as the messenger. I hope that person seeks help, too.

When I rewind the clock and go back in time, I notice certain things about me that I feel unable to explain to myself, like why everyone thinks I am so strong while I feel so weak inside. I have doubts about every decision-making process I go through. I have learned through the years that I need to be alone at times to really evaluate my decisions. My biggest hurdle, in my opinion, has always been my inability to handle emotions; that is the one thing that I am most aware of now. I don't believe I knew how to love people properly with the same respect that I sought. That is a very hard thing to admit; I have been lucky that I have endured while staying strong with bipolar disorder for many years.

Also, as critical as I am on everyone, I am relentless with the self-criticism, so I continue to torment myself, although not as badly as I used to. It's hard to be sitting here, knowing I will never be totally satisfied with my efforts, that there will be flaws in my work. I will get over it, as I always do. I think my dad passed on this trait to me. No matter what I do or have done, it is never good enough; I have failed lots in my life. However, I also have succeeded lots; my greatest accomplishment is my children. They have definitely made my life worth living each and every day. I have had more good thoughts thinking about Angela, Deirdre, and Cassie, throughout the years, to release the bad thoughts tenfold. Whenever I get depressed, I think of my children; even though they did not live with me, they were always with me and kept me strong.

I recently asked my psychiatrist, "Why can I be so nice to people I don't know while being such an asshole to the people who I love the most?" He laughed for a second and told me I needed another shoulder. I understood what he meant, but I did have to think about it for a while. When I look back at my marriages, I see all the same traits, where I don't know how to treat my partner properly. I take full responsibility in all my relationships for that trait. Hell, I wouldn't want to live with me, either. Now, I'm not saying I'm an asshole all the time, but I have taken things way over the edge on numerous occasions. Not just to the people I have been married to—my children have also felt the brunt, as well as Corinne's son, Daniel, and Melanie's son, Evan.

I remember Daniel as a young boy; I think he was about six when I first met his mother. He had his mom and grandma wrapped around his finger. He was a good kid, did well in school, and kept his nose clean. He was not into sports but loved playing Nintendo; he was good at it. I would practice at night to get to the same level as him. Many nights, I was frustrated that I couldn't get to the level he was on. Daniel was a natural musician who enjoyed making music of all kinds; he also played saxophone and piano. He also did computer music where he wrote songs. I embarrassed Corinne one night at parent-teacher interviews when I got into an argument with Dan's teacher over math. The teacher and I went at it pretty well. I was never invited to go back for another interview after that. I know that Daniel had issues with me for a long time; maybe he should have. I was hard on Dan to make him a man while making him take responsibility for his actions when he was thirteen or fourteen. One day while I was at home, the school had phoned looking for Dan. He had skipped school; you can guess what happened. I hope Daniel took some of the lessons I taught him back then and is doing well for himself now.

Evan was a momma's boy right from the start; in fact, it would not surprise me if Melanie still tucked him in at night now at age eighteen. There is no malice intended in that comment, but I do know his mother. Evan was also the product of divorce; he had a hard time with his dad being so far away, as he didn't see him all that much. Evan was a tremendous artist with the talent to draw anything he wanted. Also a musician, he took up guitar right before I left the house. Evan will also learn from the lessons I taught him throughout the years.

I have just brushed the surface with my children and stepchildren; they have all been a very important part of my life. I regret that all of you were hurt by divorce; for that, I am sorry. There are many things that I remember fondly about each of the children; however, I did not pursue a relationship with Daniel and Evan after the marriages broke up. I sometimes wonder if I should have, but really, they were old enough to pursue that avenue as well if they had wanted to.

So really, what would you think if you were forty-five years old, divorced three times, bankrupt three times, unemployed, and starting over again? Well, that's where I'm at now. All in all, when I look back on my past, it wasn't all that bad; there were an awful lot of good times as well. When thinking of bipolar disorder, please don't assume it's all doom and gloom all the time, because it's not. We seem to focus on the doom and gloom because that is what is the hardest to handle. Also, getting the right professional help can do wonders. Treatment is ongoing and should be followed. I know that I am the world's worst for going to the doctor with something wrong, getting a prescription, then, after I am feeling better in a few days, not taking the medication. This does not work in mental health; you cannot be the doctor; you must follow your doctor's directions.

If I had a magic wand, I would wave it everywhere and stop all the illness, disease, pain, and suffering of every human being on earth; then, I would be quickly shot for doing it. Being sick is big business for doctors, pharmacies, and drug companies, for they could not exist if people were not sick. Don't kid yourself; just think how much is spent on drugs alone: it's in the billions. Each day, someone somewhere is told that his or her life is almost over, or he or she has a terminal illness. The two illnesses that I face will not kill me unless I let them; yes, I am unlucky to have both of my conditions, but I see it as lucky that with the proper treatment, I will not die anytime soon. I can accept that any day.

Melanie's brother-in-law Larry was a good friend to me; we bowled together with our wives, had a few beers together, laughed lots. We talked hockey, kids, plus everything in between. I was visiting Angela at the coffee shop where she worked on Fridays; then, she dropped the bomb that Larry had passed away about six months before. I was shocked; it shook me up pretty well. Larry was only in his early fifties, had worked his whole life to enjoy his retirement that he was going to take early. I had hired his son, Adam, to work with me at Cascade for the summer; then, Larry helped Angela get a job at Zellers. It really upset me to hear he had passed away suddenly; his lifelong dream would not be achieved. I realized how precious life really is that day as I mourned his loss.

On October 6, 2007, we celebrated Jacob's first birthday with a party at Deirdre and Curtis's home. It was something like a reunion for me as Charlene was there, along with her parents, Ken and Janette. Heather and I had a great time watching all the children play. Jacob was walking really well; he was checking everything out. There were quite a few people as Curtis had his family, also; I was able to visit with everyone, so that was nice. I went outside to have a smoke while Charlene was there having one; we talked for quite a while about mental illness and about Angela and Deirdre. We were both very proud about the girls' achievements and where they were in their lives.

I know that as parents, we did what we could for our children, even though we were divorced; there was no baggage, so we worked together to get things done while not involving the children in our squabbling when it did happen. Charlene and I made a pact when we first got divorced that we would not bad mouth each other in front of the children, so we didn't. I enjoyed Jacob for the rest of the time we were at the party; I always wondered why my dad was so different around my children than he was around me as a kid. Now, as a grandparent myself, I have figured it out, so it does make sense to me now. It is one of those questions that you can't understand until it happens to you.

Jacob is well on his way to doing anything that he wants in life, as his parents are committed to his welfare and upbringing. I am looking forward to the day that I can spend more time with Jacob; it has been a joy to have a grandson, but it has been hard, too, living so far away.

I remember when I was about eighteen or nineteen, I went to a dermatologist about my skin; then, he told me I shouldn't have children because the chances were pretty good I would pass it on to them. I was devastated, crying while I told Charlene about the news (this was before we were married). Charlene, in her delicate way, told me everything would be okay, not to worry, that we would get through things. That was Charlene; we did, and we also brought two fabulous people into our worlds that have a huge impact on our lives. I am glad that she assured me that everything would be all right, because I cannot imagine life without Angela and Deirdre.

The year was 1990; I met Corinne in a whirlwind romance; we were married after only three months. I was adamant that I did not want any more children, none. Then, Corinne shocked me one day by telling me she was pregnant. I accepted the news and was supportive while also being reluctant. Cassandra was born a day after my mother's birthday. Children thrive in a loving environment, and Cassie was doing well. Corinne has always been an excellent mother to Cassie, even if I think sometimes she goes overboard. I have always supported Corinne's decisions while knowing that Cassie's best interests are being looked after.

Corinne and I have had words a few times; however, since we divorced, we have no baggage; we only share the best interests of Cassie. We can be supportive of each other but also agree to disagree.

I am privileged to have three beautiful daughters who are all unique in their own ways. I respect Charlene and Corinne as the mothers of my children; also, I feel blessed that we were able to work out our differences out as adults. I have been married and divorced three times with no baggage; how lucky is that? I have friends that can't make a clean break; they have all sorts of baggage. That's no way to live; let the bullshit go and get on with your life. Love your children; then, for God's sake, take care of them.

Bipolar disorder certainly played a factor in all three divorces; however, in the first and second marriages, I didn't know I was bipolar. Corinne and I were divorced before I had my breakdown; we were living together with the intention of getting remarried someday. The thing I have to admit here and now is that every time there was an issue in all three marriages, I wanted to bail. That's right; I did, and eventually, I did in the first two, while with Melanie, she got tired of me saying I wanted out and showed me the door. Heather would hear none of that when I started that with her. One night, she told me I couldn't make that decision, as I was mentally unstable at the time. I went to see my counselor the next day, and then was admitted to the hospital. I regret no one knowing about my illness in the past; it is not an excuse, but rather, an explanation that I have gained valuable insight into my trends.

Charlene, Corinne, and Melanie were all good people; it's just that I didn't know how good I had things. I realize that I wanted to be married while living the single life, which was a bad trait of mine. Also, work came first for me. I worked hard, but I played harder, always into sports and drinking. While I was drunk, each one of them saw the nasty side of me. Corinne, I would say, dealt with that the most. Again, I'm not making an excuse; she put up with a lot of shit that she shouldn't have had to. I am glad to say that at this time in my life, I very rarely drink, and when I do, I limit myself to only a couple of beers. At forty-five, I have finally gotten some sense and copped myself on.

When I travel to Edmonton, I enjoy going to Sherlock's with Angela and Deirdre for a pint. We always have a laugh, as we know lots of the people there. The girls always keep me laughing, even though they make me feel old, ha ha. It is bittersweet to see your children all grown up with lives of their own now, even having children of their own; man, no wonder I have no bloody hair.

It has been very hard for me to deal with not having Cassie in my life, especially knowing how I caused her pain. That said, I have hope that the situation may change. You have to do everything in your power to have more good days than bad ones. You have to train your mind to think positively, as well as be positive. Let's face it: how many people really want to get out of bed when it's thirty below to go to work? None. But we all have to make a living, then pay the bills. Every day that I wake up is a good day now; what I do with the rest of the day is what makes it special or not. Keeping myself busy is one of my greatest rewards, as I feel as if I accomplish something. Doing things I enjoy also helps; my piano has been getting a regular workout lately, as I'm writing new songs. It is always rewarding for me to express my thoughts through music; it is definitely my true passion. I enjoy it immensely, while never getting tired of playing.

Not taking anything away from my girls, I would like to tell you about Heather's children, as this chapter is all about kids in my life. Her oldest son, Cody, turned fourteen on December 4, 2007. He lives with his brother, Robert, who is eleven, at their dad's in Kelvington, Saskatchewan. It is an hour and a half drive from Humboldt. Travis and Tyler are eight and live with Heather and me here, in Humboldt. When I first moved to Humboldt, all four kids were living here. Cody had behavioral issues and we clashed all the time. He did surprise me by delivering the Star Phoenix newspaper every morning and getting himself out of bed at 5:00 AM to do the job. I never figured that Cody would last, especially in the winter, but he did; the cash he made kept him feeling good. Then he really shocked me by joining cadets. Cody was very respectful of his uniform and enjoyed going to cadets every week. I felt sorry for Cody as I noticed that he was torn between his mom and dad but really didn't know where he fit in. He resented me even though I was only out for his own good, but I can understand that, as he wasn't the man of the house anymore.

Robert was my golden boy; I put him on a pedestal and made him the model child. He is funny, smart, and treats people with respect. He likes playing on the computer but hates spelling, loves soccer, and is a very lovable kid. Robert likes to stir the pot, then sit back and watch; he enjoys practical jokes, just your normal eleven-year-old kid.

I was disappointed back in February when the kids came home from a visit with their dad. I mentioned divorce and baggage earlier; well, Heather and her ex (Brian) have lots. They would not even talk without an argument, then off to the lawyers. It was ridiculous that the four children had more sense than their parents. When I came on the scene, I arranged more visitations for Brian with the boys. I mentioned to him that I was the only friend he had around there, so he shouldn't screw it up.

Heather and Brian used a communication book on the advice of the court that was swapped back and forth on each visit. On that visit in February, there were two letters—one from Cody, the other from Robert—inserted in the book regarding the reasons why both children wanted to live with their dad.

Heather was very upset with all of this; she was livid, to be honest. We discussed the situation, then decided to call Brian to make arrangements for him to pick up Cody and Robert at the halfway point.

This was one of the hardest decisions I ever had to make. I can't imagine how Heather felt; however, the situation could not go on as it was. There was constant tension in our home with the bad attitudes getting far too much attention. The first few weeks were the hardest to accept and understand what had happened. I felt like I was losing it: I couldn't sleep; I was worried about Heather; to be honest, I felt as if I had broken up another family. Really, what happened, though, is it brought peace to our house. When Cody and Robert come to visit us now, it's great; there's no bullshit. It did take a while to get to that point, as Heather browbeat the boys every time she saw them before. She has accepted the fact they are happy with their dad and that's where Cody and Robert want to be. They are welcome to come back to our house when they want with some stipulations; they are fine young men who have been caught up in the baggage of divorce. I will tell you this much, I would do anything for those kids; all they have to do is ask. Brian and I have talked; I have given him shit because the kids are missing too much school. I have told him to step up and be a dad, as that is what he wanted. Also, there is no more baggage with Heather and Brian; it's amazing what a guy with some common sense can get done. I don't believe in bullshit, as I have been shovelling it my whole life. Common sense can take a person a long way, but stupidity can bury him or her. Unfortunately, the children suffer the most from this and frankly have a hard time coping with the insanity that their parents are putting them through. Just because moms and dads don't love each other anymore, don't expect the children to feel the same way.

As a parent, my job was to raise my kids to be responsible people while being a father, not a friend. When my children were adults, we became friends. With bipolar disorder, this was a hard task to do; what I mean is that there were days that I was in the black hole of depression, and I was pushing kids to get things done while I could do anything myself. I felt a lot of guilt while I was doing this. I can't explain it other than I beat myself up for expecting too much. Yes, I did set the bar high for my children; it's still high, even now, with the boys; by the way, the bar is high for me, too. I realize now that it is hard for people to really understand my methods of thinking when I am going through an episode of depression or mania, and that's okay, because I don't, either. I know my triggers and try to avoid them at all costs now that I am a bit more sensible. My triggers for a bout of misery are as follows: too much stress, no job, too much time to think (usually gets me manic), no money, dealing with idiots, prolonged cold spells, along with the extended darkness of winter. City driving is one thing I just get pissed off at every time I have to do it, so I don't much anymore, thank God.

The following poem is what inspired me to really get going on this project. My daughter Cassandra always inspired me with her talent, and now, I really hope that I can inspire her with mine. Life is hard, sure, but you have to see the light and follow it. God put me on this earth for a reason. I am but one person—in a world of billions—that understands everyone has problems and that everyone is important. Sure, we get lost along the way in this journey of life, but we have to realize that life is precious. Being bipolar is not the end of the world; yes, it's a challenge; it can be devastating; however, for me, it is a sign of my character and who I am. Never give up, always try and never lose hope, be inspired, and lose your self-doubt. If you are bipolar, keep your chin up. If you're family, please be patient; sometimes, we don't understand what's going on. I hope that sharing some of my experiences may make you think about what's important in life. Some of the most compassionate and understanding people in the world work in the mental health field; never be afraid to utilize their talents

Bipolar Shoes

By Dave O'Riordan

It's a different way of walking life when you must be encumbered
or when your body is awake and your head is still in slumber.
As depression has its turn and really does a number,
These bipolar shoes are just my day-to-day lumber.

These shoes are kind of awkward, not to mention really tight.
When your head is in ten places and you get no sleep at night,
relaxing is impossible, so I use the time to read or write.
These bipolar shoes are just my day-to-day plight.

Jen, my therapist, is very dedicated to her vocation.
She ties my shoes up right so they won't give me frustration.
I appreciate her efforts in understanding and salvation.
These bipolar shoes are just my day-to-day sensation.

Every time I wonder how this illness affects my tenure,
I'm up, I'm down, or I'm round and round; it's really quite a venture.
I say a little prayer to God, and he helps me see the picture.
These bipolar shoes are just my day-to-day adventure.

Someone somewhere else, has been diagnosed with bipolar shoes.
They find them quite uncomfortable as they're dealing with the news.
I want to tell them about this life and share my points of view.
These bipolar shoes are just our day-to-day reviews.

Chapter 4

People Are People

So far, I haven't made much mention of my mother; that's because I really have a hard time putting into words the effect she has had on my life. I know I love her very much; I, as well as most people, tend to focus more on the negative aspects rather than the positive ones, and that's not right, but it is human nature. As with everyone in this world, all to often I blame other people for things that they can't help doing, as they know no better. This is the case with my mother. In the years since Dad passed away, I have become very close to Mom as I have always thought of her first; she has taken good care of me, too. Mom doesn't drive and never has, except for a few lessons she took when she was younger. So she needs to get out for groceries and run errands; as such, I always made myself available to run her around.

Mom has always been in my corner, pushing me in the right direction to see the positive side of life and kicking me in the ass to get moving and get out of my funk. Sometimes, it has been hard to accept, but it is her way of trying to make me see what's going on. There were times, however, that no matter what she did or said, I would get pissed off and think she was interfering with me. But I think that probably went both ways; a love I shared with no one was always there for the taking, and we did have a nice life together for the most part. Mom helped me out lots throughout my life and always had kind words of encouragement to get me through some really tough situations. Now, I do believe in my heart that Mom suffers with bipolar disorder, as she shows lots of the traits. I have amassed information for her and everyone else to review.

In learning about bipolar disorder, I have gained the knowledge that it runs in families and that many people never get diagnosed with the illness. The following information I obtained from http://www.bipolar. com. This is just information. If you think some of these symptoms are bothersome, please do get help; your husband of wife may thank you. Bipolar disorder is not the end of the world, but it will change your life and kick your ass if you let it.

Symptoms of depression include

- Feeling sad or blue, or "down in the dumps"
- Loss of interest in things the person used to enjoy, including sex
- Feeling worthless, hopeless, or guilty
- Sleeping too little or too much
- Changes in weight or appetite
- Feeling tired or having little or no energy
- Feeling restless
- Problems concentrating or making decisions
- Thoughts of death or suicide

One person describes *depression* this way:
"I doubt completely my ability to do anything well. It seems as though my mind has slowed down and burned out to the point of being virtually useless. [I am] haunt[ed] ... with the total, the desperate hopelessness of it all ... others say, 'It's only temporary, it will pass, and you will get over it.' But of course they haven't any idea of how I feel, although they are certain they do. If I can't feel, move, think, or care, then what on earth is the point?"

Symptoms of mania include

- Increased energy level
- Less need for sleep
- Racing thoughts or the mind jumping around
- Being easily distracted
- Being more talkative than usual or feeling pressure to keep talking
- More self-confidence than usual
- Focusing on getting things done, but often completing little
- Risky or unusual activities to the extreme, even if it's likely bad things will happen

One person describes *mania* this way:
"The fast ideas become too fast and there are far too many ... overwhelming confusion replaces clarity ... Your friends become frightened ... everything is now against the grain ... you are irritable, angry, frightened, uncontrollable, and trapped."
Hypomania is a milder form of mania that has similar but less severe symptoms.

This is useful information that has been provided by this Web site; it is the same as the information provided by the Canadian mental health association. I have studied and analyzed this data for many years and have come to the conclusion that my mom has an awful lot of these traits. Now, my mom is seventy-two years old, and I'm sure as hell not going to tell her she is bipolar; after all, I am not a doctor and not qualified to do so. That said, I will give examples to explain why I feel this way. It is not to rake my mom over the coals as much as it is a fishing experiment for myself to try and obtain some insight as to why I have this illness. The skin disorder that I also have is another illness that is hereditary, but I have no family member that any one of my relations can recall with this condition, either.

Mom put too much responsibility on me at a young age by making me her sounding board for her problems with Dad. She all too often uttered the words that she would be better off dead in those conversations; as a child, I didn't think I needed to hear those comments. I feel bad that she felt that way, but really, what could I do as a kid about the situation?

Mom suffered with depression for many years off and on and had a hard time sleeping and was down in the dumps quite a bit. I do feel that she brought a lot of her issues on herself by being a gossipmonger and pitting family members against each other by talking about everyone behind their backs, being manipulative with information and facts. Mom never had a nice word to say about anyone in the family, and then she would backtrack when she was confronted. Also, she moved house over thirty times in thirty-five years while spending money like it was going out of style. Then, moving back to Ireland to no one but her brother, Martin, in my opinion, was a risky endeavour.

Now, I have to say that Sandra and Paul have always considered me the pet of the family, as Mom and I were always very close. I know her very well, and she does know me better than most people do. I have had some battles with Mom over the years, but we always do patch it up and get over it. I moved into a house with Mom after much thought. I decided this would be good for both of us, as I was paying a fortune for rent and she was paying a lot for rent as well. Mom put the down payment on a nice duplex that we both liked, and we were able to obtain a mortgage neither one of us would have obtained on our own. We now had a home together, with the understanding that I would live in the basement so I could have my privacy and that we were working together to make ends meet while sharing the expenses.

In this time, I learned a lot about Mom, as we did spend so much time together. I was also traveling lots to meet Heather and the boys. Almost every second weekend, I would go to Humboldt; on occasion, Heather would travel to Edmonton. I remember the first time Heather came, and Mom asked me if I was going to make up the sofa bed for her. I laughed and said, "I'm forty-two years old; why would I do that?" Then I laughed again, but I also understood she did not approve of this. The relationship with Heather was going very well, even though it was a long-distance encounter. I had done something with this relationship that I really had never done before, and that is to really get to know the person and her true self before I took the plunge into marriage. I was very proud of myself for this. I coped and accepted what we had developed, even though we could not be together all the time.

Mom knew of my feelings for Heather, as we talked about the situation often, and she would tease me on a daily basis and tell me I was crazy. I would spend hours every night talking to Heather, and Mom would make comments in fun. I liked the fact that she genuinely liked Heather, then went out of her way to make her feel at home when Heather did visit. This was a relief for me, as Ma didn't like anyone else I was ever involved with. I remember the first time my mom told me she loved me; that, I can recall, was my first wedding, when she said, "I love you and I hope you have done the right thing." For me, that is a lousy memory. Living with Mom was not easy, as she had her ways of getting what she wanted by making you feel guilty for not accommodating her requests. I learned to talk to my mother in a way that she understood what I was saying, even though I knew it would hurt her feelings. Marriage wasn't this tough or complicated; however, I did not give up on this mother-and-son relationship.

It was difficult for me to see Mom existing as she did; she had health problems and no real life except for the television. I would take her out on a regular basis, just to get her out of the house and to socialize with people, so she would not have time to think about the negatives in life and could start being more positive. Mom was good at giving advice but not so good at following her own wisdom; that was never so clear as the night I confronted her about her mother. As her son, I had a hard time with the pity parade she was performing. She was going on and on about no one coming to see her, that nobody cared whether she was dead or alive, so then I dropped the bomb on her about her mother, my Nan. She did not take kindly to me making a mention of the fact that she left Nan on the other side of the world a month after her dad passed away, and I asked for justification as to why that happened. I personally did not feel good about saying what I needed to say for many years; in fact, it made me break down in tears with all the emotion I had pent up about that situation for so many years myself. We finished talking; I gave mom a hug and kiss, told her I loved her, and put that episode behind us, never to see the rerun again.

I was born an Irishman, and there are certain privileges that come with that honor; first and foremost is the ability to forgive and never forget. That's right; I don't forget, but I certainly forgive. Another is to passionately express yourself in situations where you believe the only course of action is to voice your opinion and challenge the establishment. I, for one, am very proud to be an Irishman with the knack of expressing myself passionately, with conviction and humour that is honest to a fault. These traits are not tied to mental illness in any way but do get the establishment's attention. Passion is not a fault; in fact, it is a valuable piece in the foundation of humankind. With passion, I believe anything is possible; I was blessed with many other fine attributes that are unique to my structure that allow me to become more experienced in dealing with mental illness.

The stigma of mental illness still exists in society today, mainly because of ignorance of the facts. The main reason is that people don't understand or fail to educate themselves about the nature of the illness, and really, why should they? It doesn't affect them. I feel that if you can understand the mechanics of why things happen, you can deal with issues in more of a diligent manner, regardless of the diagnosis. The biggest problem that I see is that people think mental illness is a weakness and an issue most people would rather not discuss; therefore, a stigma has developed. Personally, I don't have an issue talking or telling people what has happened to me with regards to my illness and how I have learned to cope with the many facets of day-to-day living. Anyone who claims mental illness is for weak people is full of shit. It is a form of strength, the way I see it, as some of the alternatives are a lot easier and have instant results.

Granted, to take one's own life is a way to deal with the illness and in most cases is considered a definite sign of weakness. Yes, people diagnosed with bipolar disorder do commit suicide, and that is why you can never compare one person to another when it comes to this illness; each person is different, even if they have the same illness. I can only speak for myself with regards to this, and I came to the conclusion that living life was my only option, as I didn't want to put this label on my children as I stated earlier. I do, however, understand why people think this is the only way out to solving their problems. I will not judge their actions, and I would be lying if I said it was weakness. I personally think desperation would be one of the more fitting explanations.

This book project is an idea, which I have had for many years, with the intention of cleansing the pain of living with the madness and being a valuable resource to people who, like me, deal with this illness every day. I have accepted my fate with the two incurable disorders that God has blessed me with and learned to live with both, even though there is pain and uncertainty with each of them every day. I do not wish to complain, but rather, express my acceptance of bipolar disorder and Darier's disease while not pointing the finger at anyone. I am responsible for my own actions and use integrity to manage my illnesses accordingly, as I never want a repeat of the earlier breakdown I experienced.

Oprah Winfrey recently had two shows about bipolar illness that I watched with interest as the guests expressed their opinions on the topic. I personally felt that this was a great start to making resources and information available to people who want to learn about this illness with the sheer audience numbers of her show. I know that all too often in families, the understanding of mental illness is not there among family members who don't live day to day with the illness. It does not affect their everyday lives, so they don't feel the need for information. Sandra and Paul fit this category for me; neither one of them quite understands what the illness is all about, and really, I can't blame them; if I didn't have the illness, I wouldn't know about it, either.

"People Are People" is the heading I picked for this chapter, as there are so many people who have touched my life in a positive way. One of the stigmas of mental illness is that people think you are out of touch with reality all the time, and this is the farthest thing from the truth. Sure, I have my moments that are off the wall, but that is thinking outside the box, in my opinion. I love a challenge and enjoy putting my perspective on things, even if it is obscure; that's how things can get done. Sure, I do stupid things but never in a way to harm my family; the last obscure thing I did was get drunk, which I don't do a whole lot anymore. I was walking home, feeling pretty good; I walked into a tree. That put me on my ass quicker than I could say excuse me; then, I got up promptly, ran into his brother, two feckin' trees in one night; my ego was bruised, but I did laugh a lot. So did Heather; it was her first time seeing me drunk. This was in April of 2007 after a night of music trivia.

I made the decision in May 2006 to make the move to Humboldt to start a life with Heather. I gave my notice to Ashland and believed I had it all figured out. I talked to Mom about the house, and she was going to stay on for a while and make it work. She had me come up to Edmonton a few weeks later to sign the title back to her, and her lawyer gave me a check for two thousand dollars. I knew what was up; I would get paid off a couple thousand dollars; then, she would sell the house we bought for a hundred and fifty thousand dollars together, and on her own, she would sell that property for two hundred and eighty thousand dollars, a difference of one hundred and thirty thousand dollars; that made me just want to puke. I was upset for a while, but I have gotten it out of my system; once again, I forgive, but I'll never forget. It's only money; you can always make more money. It just really hurts getting screwed by your mother. It is behind me now, never to be talked about again. Mom is now living back in Ireland. I talk to her a couple of times a week on the phone.

In all my years of dealing with adversity, I have gained lots of knowledge on coping tools. In earlier years, I would have probably beaten the shit out of someone or gotten revenge; someone once said the pen is mightier than the sword, and it has taken me forty-five years to draw that sword to actually use it with compassion and love. My mom has no idea the pain and hurt she has caused everyone in my family, including me, by the actions she keeps taking without regard for anyone else's feelings except her own. We all accept her and love her, but she still is very frustrating, albeit she still is our mother.

People get comfortable in their surroundings and don't like to change. Just think of this: thirty years ago, I would not have had the opportunity to connect with you in a book, as I wouldn't have had the ways or means or education to do so. But today's society makes anything possible for anyone willing to take a chance on him- or herself. My education has not improved; it is still at a grade nine level, but I can succeed no matter what I try to do. It's called determination; it doesn't cost a lot to have determination. Hard work is a good start, a willing attitude to do your best: frankly, these are tools I had in my toolbox, but I must have lent them out. I have recovered all of these tools since I seriously took on this project. Pride, faith, and hope are wonderful friends to work with every day. People are my passion, always have been, and always will be, as everyone has his or her own story. I always enjoyed Cork City as a kid, because people would always say hello; of course, there were a few that would tell you to shag off, too. The stories were magic, and I always had a laugh.

My sister dropped a bomb a few years back that she and her husband, Mardy, were getting divorced. I have to say, it surprised me, as I always thought they were the model couple for marriage. You know me: three wives and still can't get it right. I have to look up to someone, and Sandra and Mardy were my choice for the perfect couple. Their children, Kimberly and Mathew, took it well, and Sandra and Mardy have stayed friends. It just goes to show there are no guarantees in life anything can happen to anyone.

Paul and Gerry celebrated their seventeenth anniversary back in July; they took a trip to Australia as a family after all being back in Ireland a couple of years before. It brought back memories for me about all the traveling we did as a family when we were young. They had a wonderful trip and enjoyed the sights. Emma and Declan are getting very grown up now. They are young adults; Declan is playing goalie in hockey, taking on the role of goalkeeper of the family. His granddad's Auntie Sandra and his dad were all good goalkeepers in football (soccer). Gerry has given up her teaching job; I guess I told her too many stories about mental breakdowns. She didn't like my description of the padded rooms, by the sound of it.

I often laugh when people ask me to describe myself; it is not to insult them that I laugh, but a feeling that I can only describe as awkward. Now, I can do it and have done it all my life, but really, it's not in my comfort zone—describing myself, that is. You see, it's hard to describe someone you really don't know yourself. Remember the movie *The Wizard of Oz*? Well, that's kind of what I feel like: I have all those characters inside my head, the Tin Man looking for a heart, the Lion looking for courage, the Scarecrow looking for a brain, and Dorothy looking for a way home. I can relate to these characters, as they all look for help in finding their way. I, too, look for help as I battle myself, trying to cope with day-to-day life with a mental illness and a rare skin disorder called Darier's disease. I have developed coping mechanisms to battle both of these disorders, but I also require medication daily to sustain a level balance and a somewhat normal way of life. Now, let me tell you this: I have no idea what a normal life is, but I can be happy. I do know that, and I look forward to being there again soon. In the last year, I have made wholesale changes to my life, some for the good, some for the bad.

The good is that I followed my heart; in June of 2006, I moved from Edmonton, Alberta, to Humboldt, Saskatchewan, to make a long-distance relationship with my best friend Heather and her children. It has been a struggle for us, but we are getting stronger every day. The bad is that I did it without properly researching what the job market was and buying a house before I moved here. Also, I didn't research what help was available to people who suffer from bipolar disorder. I gained a family but lost my comfort zone and support system; it takes time to build a new one.

Today, I start a new journey with my destination being wellness; I know I can't do it alone, but with the help and my trust of doctors, councillors, and family, I believe I can make my greatest comeback ever while saving myself from a life of misery along with unhappiness. I have just spent the last couple of weeks trying to cope with life after I voluntary admitted myself into the hospital for a week because of depression. I believed my world was falling apart; I had given up hope on everything, even the things that meant the most to me. I was negative about everything. I just didn't care then; I asked myself, "Why is this happening? I'm taking my medication." I had just come off a manic high and knew I was now in the depression stage.

Bipolar disorder, or as we older people call it, manic depression, is an affective mood disorder. It can occur at any age. It happens more to women than men, according to statistics, but really, who knows, as so many go undetected? Without treatment, the symptoms can last for months, years, or even a lifetime. Many people with bipolar disorder or depression do not seek treatment because their symptoms are not recognized. They blame it on personal weakness or mask it with alcohol or drugs. Maybe misdiagnosed or wrongly treated anyway, only one in three people with mental health disorders will seek qualified help. Some accompanying problems experienced as a result of a mood disorder are anxiety, panic attacks, confusion, violence, damage in relationships with family and friends, interference with work or school. Or how about feelings of sadness or hopelessness or doom and disaster, poor concentration, increased or decreased sleep, feelings of unrealistic self importance, rapid and unpredictable emotional changes, racing thoughts, anger, irritability, impaired judgment, excessive and prolonged feelings of elation or thoughts of suicide?

I have been in many battles in the course of my life, but battling myself has definitely been the hardest. Life is hard enough without constantly wondering if you've done the right thing. The easiest way I have explained my illness to people is to be honest about it; I don't shy away from discussing issues or telling the truth. People have admired me for my courage and heart and also my brains, for being strong enough to seek help when I need it. What happened was when I was diagnosed as having bipolar disorder, that news changed my life. As I learned about the illness, I was able to answer lots of questions I had about myself. To be honest, it came as a relief to know something was wrong. I have never been scared of a challenge or ever one to run from a problem, so I didn't hide from this illness, either; I fight it every day. I have had some excellent people in my corner, and I keep coming out every round.

My personal view on my illness is that I have learned to manage it; definitely, there have been struggles, but there are struggles in every aspect of life that we all have to deal with. I am happy with the person I am; I am thankful for the excellent care that I have received throughout the years. I do appreciate that I can be a productive person in society. Even though I can manage this illness by knowing the warning signs for both depression as well as mania, I always keep my guard up, as I know bipolar disorder can knock me out at any time. My advice to anyone who deals with this illness or shows symptoms is to keep your head up and never be too proud to ask for help. The following is a copy of the letter I gave my counselor, Jen Denton, the mental health nurse for Humboldt, when I was in trouble and having a tough time.

May 24, 2007

Dear Jen,

A dream is but a dream until you put it into action. I have always acted on my dreams, some with good results, some with not so good. I would like to share my story with you. I believe we are all put on this earth for a reason, some to do good, some to do bad, and others to be downright evil. I often ask myself where I fit in, and I can honestly answer that I have some of all three. I feel I am good to people I don't know, bad to people who care about me, and just evil to those I should be nicest to. It's getting harder and harder to live within my scope of reality, as I am unable to focus on tasks properly. I have no enthusiasm or drive, and I am constantly irritable. I have been jumping off the radar as far as my health goes, and I'm not taking care of myself properly; this is all due to stress, as I see my world crumbling down around me.

I have been unable to get suitable employment that interests me or pays enough for me to live; I have toyed with the idea of starting my own business. In fact, I registered a company as a sole proprietor but quickly realized it would take a lot more money to make it fly than I have; also, it will take a few months to make an income suitable to live on. The business is online marketing, and the reason I like it is that it allows me the freedom of not having to deal with people face to face each and every day and to be creative. Now, don't misunderstand; I like people, but some days, people push my buttons the wrong way, and I tend to let things fall out of my mouth that really I shouldn't. I have had so much failure and misfortune in my life that I am amazed that I am still alive. People who are worse off than me, who are not afraid of anything and overcome all odds to be happy in life, inspire me.

Living with a mental illness, even though it's treatable, is tough. I say that because you always doubt yourself and your thoughts and actions. Right now, I want to be alone and go through all this stuff by myself. I have a partner, who believes in me, but I don't want to hurt her any more than I already have; she does not understand or realize what a sacrifice I am making. This is not about us; it's about my survival, and I cannot take the stress of this relationship right now. I have given up my life as I knew it to follow a dream, but my mental health cannot cope with this situation as it is now.

Jen, what I need from you today is understanding! I need you to realize that I am not mentally stable and that the warning signs for a major breakdown are there. I am having unrealistic thoughts. I am having erotic dreams, which I haven't had since I was a teen. I have had hallucinations where I have visions of things coming out of the ceiling. I have thought about suicide, but I don't want the easy way out. I want my life back. I am so tired of being stressed. I am tired of putting the people I love the most through this shit. I am a person who wants his dignity back, who is not too proud to ask for help—maybe just leaves it a bit too long.

I want to be productive and feel like my life has meaning; I don't want to be stressed out all the time about money or relationships. I would like to be able to think without having a million thoughts going through my head. I would like to be able to focus on one task without starting ten others and getting none of them done. I would like to be able to sleep and have an appetite. I would like to not feel so down and broken all the time. I hate myself the way I am now. I miss the cheery person I was. I don't want to put my family—yes, that would be the ones I want to walk away from— through this shit anymore; no one deserves this, and I love them too much to let this go on. Jen, I am scared of myself and of what I am capable of doing. Heather or the children don't need that, even though I would never intentionally hurt them. I have as-saulted a police officer when I went over the edge the last time, and the real me would never do that. A real man defends his family in any way he can, and I would rather walk away than see any more harm done. I have a couple of beers once in a while, not all the time as I did in the past, so the alcohol factor is not there. The only rational thought I have right now is that I need help. I am in a very serious condition and can't keep telling myself that everything will be okay. It won't unless I do something about it. My family in Edmonton is aware of how I'm feeling, and they are being supportive, as they always have.

71

My dreams have always been out there. I wanted to be a rock star as a kid, dreamed of being a famous sports star and many others. My dream now, however, is to be healthy; it's quite simple, yet probably the hardest I will ever attain. I, unlike most people, have always lived the dream. I was a rock star in the sense that I sang a few songs with a band on stage and got the rush on numerous occasions. I had the notoriety of the whole school when I played soccer. I was famous and had to sign autographs. I have forgotten about myself for so long, health-wise, that I don't really know where to start. So, where do I start? I know I have mental health issues and probably should start there. You and your team are the best to determine what course of action to take, and I will trust and abide by your decisions. I want to get healthy both in mind and in body. I don't want to give up. Thanks for letting me share this. I am down but not out,
Dave

I gave the above letter to Jen on a scheduled appointment. I showed her pictures of my girls and grandson, Jacob, first, and then I let her read the letter. She advised me to go home and pack a bag for the hospital. I was admitted at 5:00 PM by Dr. Vakeesen, whom I had never met before. She was outstanding, and I hit it off with her right away; she had a very understanding attitude, and I really liked her compassion. Jen understood me, and with her professional mental health training, she made the right decision on my behalf. I still see Jen a couple of times a month, as she is a very valuable asset to my team of health care professionals. I changed my family doctor to Dr. Vakeesen after that hospital stay. I requested that she accept me as a new patient, which she did, and we have an excellent patient-doctor relationship; she was able to get me a psychiatrist appointment in two weeks that my former doctor could not have gotten anytime soon. Now, don't get me wrong; I have to get aggressive with people to make things happen and get things done sooner rather than later. The following email I sent to my brother and sister the same day as I gave Jen the letter.

Sandra and Paul, May 24, 2007

I was looking out the window the other day and thought to my-self, life has to be better than this. Maybe my expectations are too high. I cannot be happy doing what I do all day or perhaps it's my mental illness sticking its head in again; I don't know. I do know that I have felt worthless and irritated a lot the last few weeks. I know myself, and for the last year, I have been stressed to the max, worrying about everyone but myself. The way my relationship ended with Mom was not pleasant and did take an awful lot out of my spirit. I was able to tell Deirdre how I felt about her and put some hard feelings to bed, and for that, I'm grateful; she is a wonderful mother to Jacob, and I am very proud of her. Angela is the kindest person I know, and I am proud to say that, because she had a rough childhood. She deserves nothing but the best, and I know she is happy in her life with Alex. Then there's Cassie, whom I haven't seen in over a year, and I don't know how she is doing; I miss her.

I am in disbelief of the mess my life is in; I don't know where to turn or what to do anymore. I need help to turn it around. I be-lieve in myself and know it will get better. Last night, I made the decision to end my relationship with Heather. Of course, she was devastated and doesn't understand. I love her, but I can't be with her, as it is just too hard for me. Right now, my financial picture is very bleak. I owe about fifty thousand and have a couple of hundred in the bank; my unemployment insurance runs out in about six weeks, and I can't afford to work for fourteen dollars an hour. I have been looking at the option of going bankrupt again. Life is not about money; it's about survival, and I know I'm one tough bastard to have put up with all the shit I've been through. I want my dignity back. I want to be productive and feel as if my life has meaning. I am hoping that both of you can help me out. First off, I need a job, and anything you both can do for me would be much appreciated. I need to get back to Edmonton, where I have contacts that can help me out, also. Tim has always been a great friend to me and is like a brother. I have nothing here to look forward to; it is nice that it is a small town, but my mental health comes first. I do not want a repeat of years ago, as I know I can't take that again.

Heather's maturity has the most to do with my decision. I just can't take it anymore, and I miss my kids. I pursued a dream that did not work out, and for that, I'm sorry, but no regrets. Heather is a good person who just doesn't understand me. Life has thrown me many curve balls, and I never give up; I won't this time, either. Now, don't get me wrong; I have thought about doing just that many times over the years, but I will never do that to my kids. I need help, not a hand out, and I want to have a life. I would be grateful if you could make life a little easier for me. Quite frankly, this is a little embarrassing, but it is easier for me to express myself this way. I have taken my reality check, addressed the issues. I have made a decision and will live with the consequences; life goes on, and I will, too. Thank you both in advance for your help, Dave

Please let me make a point: Sandra and Paul don't really have a clue about mental illness. Even though it is in their family, it is hard for them to understand, as they are not involved in the day-to-day copings of the illness. I spent seven days in the hospital in May 2007; I had my medication adjusted and started to feel better. Heather would not let me end our relationship, as she had taken up the challenge to educate herself on bipolar disorder quite a while before this. She knew this was one of my traits from past discussions with me. My major issue was the stress of not being able to find a job and knowing that my world was closing in on me. I was broke; I had spent every penny just to keep my head above water, and I was drowning fast.

While in the hospital, I decided that I had to make things work, no matter what, and my main goal was to not sink Heather and her children.

I had made what I would call somewhat questionable decisions, and one really bothered me. There were problems with the two older boys, Cody and Robert, wanting to live with their dad, and it was expressed by letters from the boys that they wanted to live with their dad when they returned from a visit one long weekend in February. I convinced Heather to let the kids go, and we drove back and met their father halfway. I knew how Heather felt about this after a couple of days, and I didn't feel good about it, either. In fact, it made me sick to where I couldn't sleep or think properly.

There is nothing worse than knowing you caused pain and grief in a family, even though Cody and Robert were doing well. I felt terrible for a long time and still have issues with the decision to separate the family. After stating that, I can comfortably state that family life with Heather was very good; sure, we had issues, but for the most part, we were happy. Again, I found myself using my old traits of bailing out of a situation when I couldn't cope with the pressure and wanting to deal with things alone; lucky for me, Heather would not accommodate that notion. We really solidified our relationship through effective communication. I also attended counselling once a week, saw my doctors, and for the first time in my life, really realized what love meant.

There have been very many people who have touched my life, some good, and some bad. I remember you all; I rarely forget a name, and I never forget a face. People are the treasure of the earth. I see only good until they show me bad. There are far more good people, in my opinion. Here's a challenge that I do every day: Say hello to people. Take the time and make the effort to say hello; you may be surprised at what you learn.

The following poem I wrote after receiving a phone call from Mom about five months after our spat in Edmonton; we had not talked for all that time and I had buried the hatchet. I have won two awards for this poem and have been told it's very personal and unique in style.

My Mom

Today you called me on the phone.
It's been a long time since we spoke.
Last time we did, some words were said
that could not be excused.

So your call today really made me feel
that time, it does march on.
And I really can't hold grudges on you,
as you always are my mom.

So today I promise to forgive
and go on with my life.
I thank you for always being there
for me throughout my life.

I hope that God can grant us time
to see each other once again.
I love you, Mom, as always.
I wish for nothing but the best.

Chapter 5

A New Way of Life

Not all things in life are bad; in fact, some things are downright magical. I have always been one to pursue adventure and take chances most people wouldn't dream of venturing into. I guess that's what makes my juices flow; it's who I am and what I enjoy.

It was a Sunday in April 2005, and I was checking out who was online with Canadian Personals that afternoon. There was a profile of a woman that caught my eye because it said she was from Snowdrift Saskatchewan; I was wondering where the hell that was. Being the curious type and never worrying about getting rejected, I sent Cinderella 67 an instant message just to say hello. Cinderella responded, and we chatted online for about an hour; she asked me to call her on the phone and I did.

I learned a lot about this person in a few short hours that first day: her name was Heather; she lived in Humboldt, Saskatchewan; she had four sons, for starters. What really intrigued me was that her background was very similar to mine. Heather's parents, Burt and Maggie, were from Glasgow, Scotland, just a wee bit away from Ireland, so we had a lot in common with each other right off the bat. Burt and Maggie immigrated to Canada with their baby daughter Pauline in 1966, and Heather was born in 1967 in British Columbia, Canada.

After my initial conversation with Heather, I was intrigued by her personality: she seemed very outgoing; she had attainable dreams and was definitely grounded. We talked on the phone and chatted online, often for hours at a time. This was new to me, as I usually met people in person; this experience was different, as I felt as if I knew Heather better than anyone, and I wasn't rushing into another doomed relationship. We made plans to meet on the long May weekend of 2005, which was hot and beautiful in Saskatoon, where we met.

It was a five-and-a-half-hour drive for me as I set out for Saskatoon from Edmonton with a pile of CDs, along with loads of anticipation, to meet Heather. It was a long drive to say the least; thank God for Tim Horton's, as I hit the one in Lloydminster and another in Battleford. I questioned myself a few times along the way about what the hell I was doing. It did feel good, but as I got closer to Saskatoon, I felt my nervous tendencies kick in. I felt a little awkward, as if I was meeting an old friend, but I couldn't remember what she looked like. I arrived at the hotel in Saskatoon at noon after making a stop at Safeway to get some flowers and a teddy bear. Heather met me at one o'clock, as we had arranged, and it was nice to finally see her and give her a hug and kiss. It was awkward during our first meeting, as we were both nervous, with neither of us knowing what to expect. We went for lunch in the hotel's Irish pub, where I promptly got into the Guinness. I had about four pints in half an hour, along with my fish and chips. I was doing all the talking, and Heather was laughing at me.

The rest of the day consisted of dropping off a TV for repair and going to Superstore for some potato seeds for Heather's mom. As we were going to Superstore, Heather almost cut off this guy going in there. I told her the guy was there, and she swerved to miss him; we both laughed. We then went for a walk on the riverbank and enjoyed spending time together. The conversation was good, the laughs were good, and the company was great. I felt very comfortable in Heather's presence; she made it easy for me to feel relaxed and be myself. I also knew I had made a good decision in coming to meet her; she was genuine and down to earth. It was very natural for me to be with Heather. I could be myself and not have to act the part that I acted so well; it was refreshing to just be Dave.

We toured Saskatoon on the second day with Heather giving me the history of buildings and landmarks. It was a beautiful day with the sun shining and people having an enjoyable time all around us. We drove out to Humboldt so I could meet Heather's mom. Humboldt is a small city in the heart of Saskatchewan with about 5,000 people living there. It is small, quiet, and friendly. I met Heather's mom, along with her friends, Linda and Rob. The time that I spent with Heather was very special; we talked lots about our lives and how similarly we were brought up. I hit it off immediately with Maggie, Heather's mom; we talked about things from our part of the world. She did razz me as I follow the Celtics and she is a true blue Rangers fan. Heather would keep looking at me with this sheepish grin that turned into this magic smile. Even though we had just met in person, it felt as if I had known her my whole life.

On Monday, we went for breakfast at the hotel with both of us having the brunch buffet. I had told Heather early on that I liked pancakes with sugar and lemon; she also liked them that way, so we both had them. The time was flying by for both of us; Heather had to be home for her boys, and I needed to drive home and get prepared for work the next day. It was hard saying goodbye to Heather; we kissed and went our separate ways, then waved to each other as I went one way, she the other.

The weekend was superb, one of the best I have ever had; in fact, I had a hard time thinking about anything other than Heather the whole way home. I knew that she was someone special who was right for me, as she accepted me for who I am. We both realized it was going to be difficult to have a relationship living as far apart as we did, but the two of us were committed to making it work. The phones got a good workout every night, as well as e-mail and live chat on MSN. I looked forward to talking to Heather each and every night on the phone; we would have some very interesting conversations that always involved laughing. Heather had some issues with thyroid cancer in her past; she had had surgery to remove half of her thyroid. Her doctor was concerned that she now had cancer on the other side.

She told me this one night on the phone; then, we discussed it at length. I decided that I would go to Humboldt for moral support; however, her boys were home, so I would have to meet them. Her oldest son is Cody, who was eleven when I met him; then, there's Robert, who was nine, and twin boys Travis and Tyler at six years old. I was concerned for Heather, but it was nice to finally meet the boys that she talked so much about. Heather and I did not spend a whole lot of time together that weekend. We did have a big soccer match on Sunday; I also spent a whole lot of time with her boys. We all had a good time. I checked out of the hotel, had supper with Heather and the kids, and then drove back to Edmonton.

Heather went to her specialist, who told her she had nothing to worry about, so she felt relieved. I could tell by the tone of her voice that she was much more comfortable now after seeing the doctor. I was delighted with the news she was all right, as I worried a lot about her. I didn't tell her I was worried, as I felt the need to support her in a positive way by not letting her think of the worst. It definitely was hard not to be there for her while she was going through all of this; however, I was in our own way. I travelled to Humboldt as much as I could; almost every second weekend, I would make that six-and-a-half-hour journey to spend time with Heather and, on some weekends, the kids.

I started to spend more time with the boys, as they were happy to see me come and visit. I then invited Heather and the boys to Edmonton for a long weekend. I took them all over the city; they enjoyed the space science center and west Edmonton mall the most. We had a good weekend with everyone having fun. Heather and I had many talks about her and the kids moving to Edmonton so we could be a family, but I had my reservations about that. I didn't feel the boys were street smart enough to make such a drastic change in their environment; also, it would interfere with visitations they had with their dad. It would make it almost impossible for them to see their dad, living in Edmonton, and as a single dad myself for many years, I knew how important it was to see my kids. I kyboshed the idea of Heather and the kids moving to Edmonton on that reason alone.

Brian Morrow is Heather's ex-husband and the father of her children. They had split up and divorced several years before we met; however, there was still a lot of baggage left on the table with the two of them. They could not communicate in regards to the children, with every issue turning into an argument or a trip to the lawyer's office. I found this quite amusing when Heather would tell me what was going on. I continued going to Humboldt every second weekend, even through the winter months, with Heather flying to Edmonton twice and driving with the children twice. We were making this relationship work as best we could.

Now, at this time, I was getting a little fed up with my job at Ashland, and to be honest, I wasn't feeling great mentally. I was contemplating my future a lot and trying to decide what was the right course of action to take.

In June of 2006, I made the move to Humboldt, Saskatchewan, to start a life with Heather and her four sons; it was a shock to the system, let me tell you. I was doing my nut trying to cope with the mayhem. It was a huge adjustment physically and mentally, and it seemed as if we lived in total chaos, shouting kids, fighting, and arguing, also being really rowdy and not doing what they were told. Now, most guys would have trouble taking up a relationship with a woman who has four boys, but then, I'm not most guys. I spent the time to get to know the boys, what they liked and disliked. I also spent a lot of time with Heather, talking about the children each night when they went to bed. The children were not my main concern, but I realized early on that whether I liked it or not, they were going to make or break our relationship.

The time Heather and I had together was precious, and we talked about everything and anything. We talked about our pasts quite a bit. I was so excited to now be in Humboldt and with her every day. The steam of my enthusiasm soon faded, as I could not get a job for love nor money. I was frustrated, and to be quite honest, I felt like a failure. I was enthused for about five months and then went in the toilet, suffering from depression, and now I was screwed. I had no support system in place in Humboldt for my mental health, and it took me a long time to get a support team together that I was confident in. It is so vital for me to be able to access professional help when I need to, and I now have the best team I have ever had for support and guidance and medical needs. This is ongoing help that I will always have to fall back on, and I appreciate the work and efforts of this team of professionals. As with anything in life, you have choices; you must have doctors and other professionals that you feel comfortable with. You are the boss, and you decide who is going to be the best for you; be picky and ask lots of questions.

Being bipolar is the most confusing, self-abusive, incomprehensible, tormenting, annoying, and rewarding illness I know of; it is who I am. There are days, weeks, and months, sometimes even years, where everything is normal and medications are doing their jobs, and then out of the blue, you get hit in the face with a shovel, and bad things start to happen. It happens with no notice, or you may have warning signs; either way, it is not like having the flu and going to bed and feeling fine the next day. I wish it were that simple; honestly, I do. I have dealt with this illness for so long and still keep learning.

The thing that bothers me the most about this illness is the fact that I hurt the people I love the most, and most of the time, I don't even realize I do it until it's too late. I am very critical of every little thing and don't mind being vocal about it. I am working very hard to rectify this problem, but Rome wasn't built in a day. Come here to me now; I don't want to get rambling on about all the bad things of this illness. Definitely, there are plusses to being in a manic state, if you are not too far over the top. This is the creative best that you can experience. I would say that all people with the illness enjoy this experience. I strive to reach a balance where I am fully functional while being productive and not too depressed. That said, I have done some very good work while I was on the low cycle and have managed to function either way. People do notice what mindset I'm in by the quality of work I produce when they really know me.

This is a double-edged sword that can really take its toll on you. For example, Dave unloaded three truckload orders in four hours today; he got everything put away and all the paperwork completed and entered into the system. That day, I was totally focused on the task at hand. Then, a week later, it took me ten hours to complete the same task, because I couldn't focus and kept making mistakes that I had to rectify because I was depressed. Everyone is then wondering what's going on with you and why your production is down so much. That's when you can't win. Days like that bury you, and they are frustrating as well. I learned how to exercise my mind to stay focused and be able to complete the task in the allotted time allowed. I also came up with a better system that made my work accurate the first time, every time.

The date now is November 5, 2007, and a lot has happened while trying to write and format this book. I have had two more stays in the hospital, a week each time, with the latest one for my skin, which was badly infected. I believe I had a reaction to the new medication I'm taking for bipolar disorder that flared this bout of misery. I have spent several chapters giving a brief summary of my life, which I believe I have done very admirably by not knocking too many people. The reason I am writing this book is for the money; that's right, I have no shame in admitting that my family and I need to survive, and I will make it happen.

To be quite honest, my story is just about a hardworking man who has fallen again on hard times and is unable to support his family. I have pride and dignity that are battered and bruised beyond recognition; however, I also have hope and faith that I will prevail again soon. Every person on this planet has a story, and like everyone else's, my story keeps growing. I would like to get you up to date now and continue with bipolar shoes.

Since I have moved to Humboldt, I have made a whopping $175.00 on two jobs, one lasting two hours and netting me $24.00. But I have to thank Bruce Bornhorst at Bornhorst Seeds in St. Gregor, Saskatchewan, for giving me a chance, even though it took me two weeks to recover from the two hours of backbreaking labor I knew I would not be able to handle. The other job was for two days at $8.00 per hour as a front desk clerk at a hotel; since I am bipolar, this was a bad choice, as the boredom was unbearable. I was very excited to get the opportunity to work, even at such a small wage; four hours into the job, I knew it was not for me. There were security issues that made me uncomfortable, and I also knew I would not like the job. I have had to file for bankruptcy for the third time in my life, and frankly, I'm pissed off about that and the fact my car was seized by the bailiff.

I have been excited over several employment opportunities here in Humboldt, but none have panned out with a job offer. I did get an offer from Koenders as a shipper, but they would not accept my counteroffer for a suitable wage. I believed I had an excellent shot at landing the shipping supervisor position at Del-Air Systems after an outstanding interview with the production manager, Colin. He called me and gave me a pat on the back for a great interview but decided to give the job to someone else. I decided to start a home business in April 2007 and did the legwork, registered as a sole proprietor with the trade name of ADC Marketing Consultants. ADC standing for my daughters Angela, Deirdre, Cassandra, and marketing consultants give me the freedom to pursue anything and everything. Realistically, it is going to take money to really get that up and going—money that, at present, I do not have, but I am going to generate. With the purchase of this book, you are getting me started, and I thank you for that. Work has always been good for me, even when I'm depressed, because I always feel a sense of accomplishment and self-worth. In doing this project, I am cleansing my own soul, telling everyone that dreams can be accomplished, while showing myself that I am worthwhile and very capable of making a difference in this world. I am still looking for work, but I'm not having a whole lot of success in that department at the moment.

My life circumstances have caused me to get way too stressed out, getting calls from collection agents looking for money I didn't have. In August of 2007, I claimed bankruptcy for the third time in my life, and it really got me down. I knew I was going to have my car repossessed. I had no money, no job, and no potential for either here in Humboldt. I was down but not out. Life has its own way of pointing you in the right direction sometimes, so while not being able to sleep, I started pecking the keys on the computer, writing about bipolar disorder and myself. I came up with the idea to approach former employers and family for sponsorship of chapters to facilitate the publishing costs, and if you are reading this, they have come through, and I thank them all. I know most people wouldn't have the balls to acquire funds this way, and again, I am not most people.

I have been robbed and tormented by mental illness, not once, not twice, but many times, and by Jesus, I would like to get something back from this unpredictable menace that I have carried around for so many years. Bipolar disorder has cost me an awful lot of heartache, as well as financial ruin over the years, and now that I'm broke and have nothing but the love of a great family, I would like to be able to give back to them in a way that I haven't been able to before. Unfortunately, love doesn't put food on the table, but a creative mind can and will.

This adventure has been good for my self-esteem, putting the hope and confidence that I lost some time ago back into my arsenal. A man somehow loses his self-respect when he cannot support his family financially, whether he suffers from a mental illness or not. Definitely, bipolar disorder is at its worst when you are down and out, but right now, for me, it's bringing my strengths to the forefront. I have the confidence and vision that my story will be told and that it will make a difference to people's lives. Hell, no, I'm not manic; yes, that is a very powerful statement to make, but I believe that it will happen. It's okay. To dream—everyone has dreams; I am living my dream now, even though some days, it feels more like a nightmare. This is absolutely not the way I had everything figured out, when I decided to move from Edmonton. I felt that with my skills and attitude toward work, I would have no problem gaining employment. Boy, was I wrong on that front; although I have never given up, it has battered my ego to the extreme. I have been blessed with the love of a beautiful woman and her kids who have never given up on me; even when I have doubted my own abilities, they have given me nothing but positive support and encouragement. Even "she who must be obeyed" (Maggie, the mother-in-law) has been very supportive.

Well, it's funny how life can change, because since I was writing this chapter, I received a phone call from Colin at Del-Air with regards to a position as a shipper, and I was offered a job, which I gladly accepted. The money isn't great, but the work is; I am happy to be back in my element, finally working again. However, I do feel bad that I cost a man his job because of my experience and commitment to making the shipping department more efficient and accountable for its actions. Yes, this was the man that the company picked as the shipping supervisor over me; I had no hard feelings about that, but the company hired me to do the job of shipping. And that I did, as well as turn the department into an efficient part of the operation by putting some urgency into the day-to-day operations of the shipping lifeline. It's amazing how a phone call can change your life; this one did just that for me, and I am truly grateful for the opportunity.

I had phoned all my family and friends the night before I had my initial interview to pray for me that I would get the job of shipping supervisor.

Well, that didn't happen; I believe that was a good thing, as I wasn't ready mentally at that time. However, when I received the call about the shipper position, I was in the perfect mental state to act on the opportunity, which I did. I am now running the department while enjoying every minute of it. My home life is a lot better now, too, so to all my family and friends, thank you for your prayers; God answered them in his own way by ensuring that I was mentally stable enough to give the job my best effort.

Okay, so I have over twenty-five years of experience in the shipping and receiving game; it is still unique with every business, as you have to learn the product. I am lucky that I can do that with little or no effort; it just comes naturally to me. I take a lot of pride in doing my job while not being afraid to make decisions to make the company more profitable and efficient. When I am at work, I am totally engaged in what I am doing, I don't think about anything other than work for the eight hours that I'm there. I cope with everything from my skin to bipolar disorder while doing my job; I suck it up and make my living. The people I am now working with are excellent. We get the job done while having a few laughs doing it. Work is not about the money for me anymore; it is about enjoying what I do, and right now, I am doing that. I am working while still writing *Bipolar Shoes*. Let's face it: I could have packed this in, but I made a commitment to myself that I would have this book published and launched in 2008, God willing.

So, I ask this question, why should I do this? My answer is simple: there are lots of people who can benefit from my years of knowledge dealing with mental illness. A few weeks ago, I was unemployed, down in the dumps, and just plain frustrated at life in general. I had no money, no hope, and no prospects that anything was going to change anytime soon. I forgot to believe in myself, my abilities, and my desire to succeed in life. Sometimes, life is hard to live, but it makes you appreciate the strength each one of us has to be able to cope with everything that is thrown at us.

I am a simple man with a lot of common sense who realizes that at the end of the day, life is not about money; it's about people. I have asked myself thousands of times what the hell I am doing on this earth or if I am making a difference in people's lives. My response is as follows: I am living life to the best of my abilities with the tools the good Lord provided me with. I never realized how much of a positive influence I have had on people by being a good communicator and teacher. I enjoy a challenge, whether it be at home, teaching the boys something new like the rules of soccer, or helping out a friend who is having some personal problems. The four words I love to hear are "it can't be done"; nothing motivates me more than hearing that phrase. Why, you ask? Well, it's like this in the story: I do not accept poor excuses, and anything can be done if you set your mind to it. Ideas and creativity make the world go around; if someone has a vision and a good plan of attack, anything can be done.

Just think of this for a second: the lady that wrote the Harry Potter books was broke and on welfare; she kept getting rejected by publishers. She had a vision that her stories were good for kids. That author is now rich beyond her wildest dreams as the sales keep soaring of her products. I don't let people shatter my dreams; I make them happen. Hold on tight to your dreams was a song that ELO put out in the eighties that has always been an anthem for me. Life is too short not to live your dreams, and the only one who can stop you attaining those dreams is you.

Being bipolar has its advantages in achieving success, because most people who know that you are bipolar already think you're full of shit. Bipolar disorder is a lifestyle, not a choice; I didn't ask to have this illness, and after having it for so many years, I don't know if I would be the same without it. I can also say that if I didn't experience my lifestyle the way I did, I would not be the person that I am today. The hardest thing for people to accept is change. With bipolar disorder, you have to change; the first thing you have to do is realize it's not the end of the world. If you are required to take medication, you had better do that, and don't stop unless your doctor tells you to do so. If you are having problems with medications, talk to your doctor; if you don't, you are not helping your situation. The first step to being successful is taking care of you. I can speak from experience that sitting around the house in your pajamas, feeling sorry for yourself, doesn't work that well, as it only gives you more time to think about your doom and gloom; also, the longer you do that, the harder it is to get out of your funk. Depression is a bitch; I know that all too well, but you can't wallow in self-pity. The first thing is realizing that you are in that phase of the illness. The thing that annoys me is when family or friends tell you you're depressed; everyone is entitled to a bad day or off day. Sometimes, you just need to rest. Also, you don't need everyone analyzing every word you say or everything you do. Life is not perfect; people make mistakes; don't let mental illness be your demise; you must be strong for yourself.

There are people with bipolar disorder who use it as an excuse, for sure. I have attended group sessions where I could not wait to get out of the meeting. I like to surround myself with positive people and live life as a giver, not a taker. I didn't like the fact that the two groups were nothing more than pity parties until I started talking. I had to liven up the sessions. I was depressed, but I left laughing every week as I blew these people away with my attitude. Yes, I have bipolar disorder, but I'm not giving up. If Winston Churchill could govern Britain while being bipolar, the sky is the limit. There are very famous people who suffer from this illness, and then there's Dave O'Riordan, born in Cork, living in Humboldt, who is finally learning what life is all about while now enjoying it and accepting the changes he made.

"Behind every good man is an exceptional woman" is what I was often told by my mother. I just had to mention that because I finally know how to appreciate the love of an exceptional woman—Lord knows I had plenty of practice. Heather came along at the perfect time in my life, and of course, I believe that everything happens for a reason. Deep down, I feel as though moving to Humboldt was the best decision I have made to date. I have had very little stress other than dealing with Heather's baggage, namely her ex-husband, Brian. It is Christmas time, and true to form, that prick is up to his antics again. He has gone to his lawyer, stirring up the shit again, but this time, he is barking up the wrong tree. I wrote the following letter to Heather's lawyer in response to Brian's affidavit.

January 8, 2008

Xxxxxxxxxxxxx
Xxxxxxxxxxxxx
Regina Saskatchewan
Canada S4P 0R7

Dear Sir,

I am writing this letter with regards to Family Matter your file xxxxxx, Morrow versus Morrow. I would like to comment and have read into court this letter on Heather's behalf, as I was named in Mr. Morrow's affidavit.

I am very much disappointed in Mr. Morrow's actions regarding his children. Since I have been involved with Heather, I have seen him constantly use the excuse that he has no money. As a father myself, I made the decision to move to Saskatchewan because I felt the children deserved to have a proper relationship with their father. I had planned on moving Heather and the children to Edmonton where I had a suitable home and excellent employment with an income of $45,000 plus pension and full benefits that Heather and the children were also entitled to.

I instead moved to Humboldt, walked away from my life as I knew it, knowing the best thing for my new family was this decision. On February of 2007, the children came home from a visit from their dad's, and in the communication book were two letters—one from Cody, one from Robert—stating the reasons why they wanted to move to Mr. Morrow's residence. Heather was devastated, and we decided the best plan of attack was to let the children live with Brian. It was arranged to do that. Cody and Robert made the decision; they also made the decisions about visitations, as they needed space. I sat down with Heather, Brian, and all four children back in November to inform Mr. Morrow that Cody and Robert had missed twenty school days. I told him it was unacceptable for him as a parent to allow his children to miss so much school. Heather kept in close contact with the school while getting regular reports.

Unfortunately, I feel Mr. Morrow uses his children as nothing more than a paycheck, because it is amazing to me that I no sooner started a job November 30, 2007, after eighteen months of unemployment, and Heather started a new position December 5, 2007, that we get this notice of motion. Mr. Morrow, the way you disappoint your children is what bothers me the most. You constantly use the excuse you have no money when it comes to picking up Travis and Tyler; you stated in your affidavit that you pick them up every two weeks. The only time you pick them up is when it's convenient for you. You get paid to come to Humboldt for your chiropractor. That leads me to another question: you are unemployed, have no real reason to live in Kelvington, so why don't you move to Humboldt to live near your children? I am sick and tired of your childish antics, like hanging up when Heather is talking. Please hang up now, and the judge can finally see what kind of a man you are.

It has cost me well over $150,000 to move to Humboldt. I have had to declare personal bankruptcy, being unable to find employment, but I had the love of a great woman that you decided wasn't important enough to give up the booze for. You have some nerve still trying to dictate her life, even though you are divorced so many years. Heather and I have had a rough couple of years, but our relationship is rock solid. I told you, Mr. Morrow, don't F--- the only friend you have around here, and you have done that numerous times in the past couple of months. I advise you to stay clear of me, as I would be only too happy to open a can of whoop ass on you. However, I am a smart man and don't want to pay the consequences of said action.

This matter before the courts today should prove what you are all about. Why are you not working? Why have you not bettered yourself in the last few years? I had a chat with Robert and Cody on their last visit and mentioned to them that they are more than welcome to come back with their mom and I. I don't want to force them, but I'm not really happy that they have you as an example. I also mentioned to them about Anne, the child you convinced Heather to give up for adoption, shortly after your marriage. You see, Mr. Morrow, you opened the door for me to write this letter by mentioning me in your affidavit. You are not entitled to any of my earnings; however, your kids are.

When I met Heather, I knew she had a deadbeat ex-husband who did nothing but cause her grief in too many aspects of her life. I fell in love with Heather and also with all of her children. Brian, your children are suffering with the pain you are causing them. I knew getting into this relationship that there would be costs incurred regarding the children, and I have no problem with that. The problem that I have is that you expect everyone to support you. Up until I gained employment, we were also on welfare. Since I am working, our rent has gone from $150 to $750; you don't hear us whine. Since Cody and Robert went to live with you, we are down $500 in child tax credit per month; do we complain? Children must be put before money. I did not see you mention once in your affidavit what you needed for the children. According to Canada child tax credits, you are getting what is allotted to you for Cody and Robert; you were able to manage before the children came to live with you. I suggest you quit smoking, sell your skidoos, and move to Humboldt. You could then partake in the upbringing of your children. Grow up and realize everyone has to work to support a family. Every father contributes money to his children. How much have you contributed in the last five years?

Children are the most important asset gained from a marriage; it is too bad that their young lives get crushed when divorce occurs. Don't make them choose between their mom and dad, because really, they can't. I have seen the pain of this divorce on all four boys; it's time for the madness between their parents to stop.

Thank You,
Dave O'Riordan

So I was on a bit of a writing spree this week, as I also gave a letter to my boss, Colin, regarding the job. I have always, in my past, taken a back seat while letting my employer decide my fate and status. At this point in my life, with my salary being so low, I felt I had to make a stand and fight for what I believe in. Now, I understand most people would not have the guts to do this, and again, I say I'm not most people. I did it with satisfying results for both the company and me. I was asked to participate in a study about transportation and how to save revenue doing it. The following is my letter to Colin.

January 13, 2008

To: Colin Hawkins

I have reviewed the outline of the RFP process while keeping the information confidential, as you requested. I have to give my honest input, which will be critical of the current process while demonstrating alternative methods, which are both cost effective as well as practical.

The key to effective distribution is having a team in place that can address issues while ultimately servicing the customers and retaining their business. Unfortunately, people who do not understand the process or the importance of timely delivery or customer satisfaction usually decide the team. I am excited to have been asked for my opinion. Colin, as you know, I have over twenty years of experience dealing with distribution and realize the importance of a reliable, conscientious carrier to be an important member of the Del-Air team. The carrier is an important part of our team; I have worked with some great transport companies over the years. I understand that some of the people driving their trucks can give a bad impression. As in any business, it is only as good as the people working for it. I am committed to the opportunity presented by Del-Air and can definitely guarantee that I can save the company at least my yearly salary in cost savings.

Now, maybe you think that is a cheeky statement, and I will agree that it is coming from a guy who has only worked for the company for five weeks. I am at home with Del-Air. I have built a reputation with many people in the company in that short time. I am honest, hardworking, and would like the monetary incentive to ensure my tenure with the company. I feel that it would be profitable for both the company and me to keep me on board and happy. I am not worried so much about the money at present; however, I would like the title of shipping supervisor to enable me to take proper control of the department. I believe it is paramount that I have the authority to delegate tasks to the rest of the team without someone feeling as though I'm stepping on toes.

Colin, I am very happy working for Del-Air; I know I have motivated people with my attitude and performance. I have developed key relationships with production that have enabled me to get orders complete and accurate before shipping. I have proven that I can learn the product quickly and I'm not afraid to ask questions. I would like a man's paycheck instead of a little boy's, and I am more than willing to share my knowledge with anyone who wants to learn. The shipping department is the heart of any production business, with ours currently suffering a slight heart attack. I guarantee that I will revive it and get it in shape for the coming busy season.

There are lots of demands made by the company about expectations of employees, some I agree with, some I don't. I believe that a person should be properly trained to function in his or her role with it being the supervisor's role to ensure this is done. I was never shown the process or how things were done on the day I started. Lucky for me, I had the experience to be able to figure it out quickly, as the supervisor I had knew about as much as the hammer on my bench about shipping. Speaking of which, he is no longer with us; I don't know what his salary was, and frankly, I don't care, but I'm sure it was more than I'm earning. I'll take that for starters, with business cards as well. You will see why I ask for the business cards later.

Yes, I am a businessman; I have negotiated many deals over the years. The biggest thing I have learned is that most companies are penny wise and dollar stupid. This, for sure, is the case with freight inbound and outbound. I have always considered the freight like what we have to be fluff. What I mean by this is that it's air: all volume, no weight. What most people don't know is that you are charged for whichever is greater, the weight or volume. If any facet of a business should be micromanaged, it is the freight and crating, as over-crating costs the company nothing but money. I have seen in my short time with the company a lot of instances where best distribution practices are not being used. I have seen over-crating, pallets not properly loaded to customers' requests, orders shipped without due care, and attention being paid to production needs. There is no point shipping one day to have the rest of the order ready the next. We are doubling the workload for our customers and ourselves, as well as incurring additional freight charges and labor costs. Also, we are setting ourselves up for failure every time we do this. For instance, I don't have all day to receive a product that is not labelled properly from our supplier. I would demand that they correct their policy and accommodate our request. I know for a fact that some of our customers cringe when our order for them comes in, as they have no idea what they're getting. I am committed to rectifying this issue.

I do not approve of throwing profit margins out the window because of overcharging by the freight designate. That does not happen when freight rates are obtained for each shipment. Also, service will improve as carriers fight for the business. I am not sure of Del-Air's procedure for reconciling freight charges, but I do know with other companies that it was not managed properly; it was ludicrous, the way it was managed. They were paying an exorbitant amount for freight until I pointed it out at a staff meeting.

In closing, there is a three-month probationary period for employees to prove their worth to the company. As stated before, I enjoy working for the company and feel I have contributed already to the reorganization of the shipping department. You now have someone who legitimately cares and has passion for results and is goal driven. It would be a shame for you to lose this diamond in the rough twice. I expect for you to announce my promotion to shipping supervisor by the end of the week and commence negotiations for a reasonable salary to compensate for my twenty-five years of experience. I am old school and respect the chain of command and do not wish to disrespect anyone. I believe in being upfront about what I want, and that is a future with Del-Air that mutually benefits both parties. I have brought a wealth of knowledge to the table and look forward to being a vital part of the organization for many years to come.

Sincerely,
Dave O'Riordan
Shipper, Del-Air Systems

Well, obviously, that letter created a bit of a stir; I had a couple of meetings with Colin where he got frustrated with me because I would not elaborate on how I could save the company money. I would not budge on this issue. At one point, he told me that if it was anybody else, he would have told me to walk, and I offered to. Now, I would not recommend this tactic to everyone; certainly, it works, but you must have the intestinal fortitude to make it work. I knew that I was in a pretty good position for negotiations but did not take for granted that the company was operating long before I got there.

I originally applied for the shipping supervisor position that paid more in salary than the position I was hired for. I looked at it as a foot in the door with nothing to lose, and now, Del-Air have created a new position just to suit me. Following is the letter distributed throughout the company by Colin after I accepted the role of shipping coordinator with a substantial raise and benefits. Of course, my responsibilities have also increased, and I'm looking forward to the challenge.

Subject: Announcement!

It gives me great pleasure to announce the promotion of Dave O'Riordan to the position of shipping coordinator.

Dave comes to us with a lengthy career in shipping, as well as experience in custom crating. These factors, along with an intense period of review within our shipping department, have removed any question that Dave is our man for the job.

Welcome aboard our team, Dave; we will be looking forward to seeing your effect in and around Del-Air Systems!

Colin Hawkins
Manufacturing Manager
Del-Air Systems/Romperland Playsystems

So all in all, I believe my letter-writing skills were very effective this week. They got results, had people talking, and made me feel a whole lot better, as I now know where I stand. Colin was a little worked up, but did compliment me on an excellent written letter and promised to frame it soon. I have always said that if you want something, go for it; the way I achieved this position is not what I would have done in the past. Before, I would have let the employer come to me; however, I have been overlooked a lot in the past. This time I was aggressive and proved my worth. This is a new way of life for me, and I am very excited that things have finally worked themselves out. I am a whole lot happier now that I am working again and now feel that I can support my family in the way I feel it should be done. Watch out, Humboldt; you have a happy-go-lucky Irishman on your hands who will be smiling and laughing lots. Thanks to Colin Hawkins and Del-Air for presenting me with an opportunity to make a living right here in Humboldt; you won't be disappointed.

I was very impressed with Colin the first time I met him back in the summer; he is a demanding manager who is very driven and committed. He can do every task in operations. Colin, however, cannot back up a semi. Use your mirrors, boss, instead of looking out the window, and you'll save us the cost of those mirrors, because I didn't see them anywhere in the budget, ha ha.

For Heather and the boys, that I got a job was a great relief. I spent months in depression and really, I guess, being like a yo-yo: up, then down; cranky, then happy; as well as losing my direction and focus. Now that it's finally over, I can say that those eighteen months were a kind of hell I never want to experience again. There were, of course, some good times with Heather and the kids, and I know if we survived that, we can survive anything. Humboldt is a new way of life, and I like it very much, thank you. It is so great not to have traffic jams in the morning, and not hearing that someone got killed the night before suits me just fine. I love my new hometown and the great people it has. I am really enjoying life again while appreciating the great things that have happened for me.

The following slogan hangs in both my work and home offices; it says it all for me.

> # *Failure*
>
> ## *Is only achieved when you*
>
> ### **give up,**
>
> ### **never try,**
>
> ### **or**
>
> ### **lose hope.**
>
> ## **So stay focused and motivated!**

While I live with bipolar disorder every day, this keeps me grounded and determined to accomplish the goals and tasks I need to complete. As I have stated numerous times, bipolar disorder is not an excuse. I have set a goal to publish this book in 2008. My fundraising effort doesn't look all that promising, as I have only had one reply. Thank you, Didi.

I received a call from my mom today, February 5, 2008; she informed me that she is moving back to Canada. She would like me to go over to Ireland and load her belongings into a container and she would pay my fare. This got me thinking: I always wondered what was wrong with me when I was a teen, as well as an adult, until I had my breakdown. I love my mom with all my heart, and I am fully convinced that she is also bipolar and can only imagine what thoughts go through her head. Of course, I will check with work to make sure I can take the time off.

When my dad died, the one wish I had was that I could go to Ireland with my mom, and again, God was listening. Also, in my poem "My Mom," I asked God to grant me the opportunity to see my mom again, and I believe that it is going to happen sooner than I thought.

In writing this book, I have learned a lot about myself and my character. I am looking forward to a happy life with my best friend, Heather. Sorry, Tim, you're now in second; by the way, Ma is coming home in April, so guess what, buddy? We have to unload the feckin' container. I guess this is move number thirty-seven; hell, you have only done about nine; might as well make it double numbers. Thanks, pally.

One Person at a Time

Life is hard to live so never take it for granted
Every person has a choice to live life how they wanted
So I can't walk in your shoes and you can't walk in mine
But together we can change the world one person at a time

So I take my medication and play by all the rules
I feel sorry for Britney Spears who's maybe got bipolar shoes
I'd get pissed at paparazzi. Get Bill O'Reilly to block the shot
I'd beat those heartless bastards 'cause a joke it's surely not

Give the girl some solitude to recover from this mess
I wish her a speedy recovery and change of attitude
Bipolar disorder is a menace to the rich as well as poor
I hope there comes a day where research will find a cure

So bipolar disorder can devastate a life that is so good
Remember one important thing that yes, you do come first
This illness left untreated will play havoc with your mood
Trust yourself and then your team to help you get the most.

**Never lose hope; remember who you are; try to make every day a good
one. Yes, you can do it !**

Chapter 6

St. Andrew and St. Patrick

I have sensed the presence of God in a few churches in my lifetime; now, I know God is supposed to be everywhere, but these feelings give you the warm tingles. The Holy Trinity in Cork was one church that gave me these tingles, with another being St. Augustine's, also in Cork, as well as the Cobh Cathedral. Ireland has many great churches that would leave you awestruck. In Edmonton, there is St. Alphonsus church where our family went out of our way to go every Sunday as the mass was beautiful with the efforts of a fellow parishioner named Albert and his music and choir. Then, there is the big cathedral in downtown Edmonton called St. Joseph's Basilica, which is also where Wayne Gretzky and Janet Jones were married.

Let's face it: there are millions of churches and places of worship for us to practice our religions, no matter what faiths we are. Personally, I feel that this is sacred and should be respected, no matter what someone else thinks. I also know a lot of people feel the same as I do regarding feeling God's presence, and that, too, is wonderful; it is a great feeling. I applied for a job at the Catholic church, St. Augustine's, here in Humboldt and decided I should probably take the nun up on her suggestion of going back to church. She had come to visit me in the hospital in May 2007, and I told her that it had been many years since I had been at church—about twenty. The sister was very pleasant and told me I should go back, so I did. Heather and I went the following Sunday; now, Heather had never been to mass, so this was different. For me, this was a cold church, no one to make you feel welcome; also, the priest was boring and just rambled on. The mass left me feeling kind of empty, especially since I can't partake in communion, as I was divorced in the Catholic church, and I would not get an annulment. Also, I did not get the job of caretaker. Heather said the same as me: that the church felt unwelcome.

Although I had not been to mass in quite a number of years, it did feel good to re-establish the deep spiritually that I had had with God. It had been a long time since I really prayed, and I needed that back. Heather has a friend named Michelle Danylchuk that is an artist who had a show at the hall of the Anglican church, which we attended. This show was superb if you are into art stuff. I thought it was neat to look at everything and get my own interpretations of what the artist was thinking, and then, I thought the show was over. In actual fact, it was just beginning; the artists told a bit about each piece of their work, and I personally found that moving. I do enjoy people's talents and marvel at how they can express themselves in their media. I, for one, could only draw a stick person, and I assure you that would not be a very good one, either. I can think it, just not do it. When the show was over, we met Reverend Beacon, who seemed like a very pleasant person, and she was not a bit pushy regarding religion.

Heather wanted to continue her quest to find a church and reminded me of the Anglican church where we had seen Michelle's show. The name of the church is St. Andrew's, and we were there on the following Sunday. The night of the show, I got the tingles and thought it was from the art, but after we were greeted at the door of the church, I got them again and realized it was God. This church is not very big in size and not decked out like some others I have been inside, but it raised the hair on the back of my neck. There is not a big congregation attending

St. Andrew's; however, everyone made us feel at home, as well as really feeling the presence of God. Heather and I were unsure about what to expect from the Anglican Church, and I soon learned it was the same a Catholic mass as soon as the service started. Reverend Beacon inspired me with her enthusiasm, and I really did hear God speaking through her in the service. After the conclusion of the service, Reverend Beacon welcomed us again. She invited us to partake in the Eucharist the next time and I explained my position with the Catholic Church and she told me those rules didn't apply in the Anglican tradition. There were prayers for the healing after the service, and Reverend Beacon took me to the front of the church by the alter and said these prayers for me. I was crying like a baby with her hand on my head, as well as Heather's and Maureen's, who is part of the healing team. The same procedure was then completed on Heather.

After healing prayers were completed, there was a get-together in the same hall as the art gallery where we formally met the congregation and had lunch together. Heather and I left the church feeling a sense that neither one of us could really describe; to be quite honest, we were overwhelmed. We discussed everything about what had happened in church the rest of the week then went again Sunday morning. We were greeted again with open arms at the front door of the church, and then took the same seat as the week before. The service began. I again felt God's presence. I was nervous about communion, as I had not partaken in the sacrament for about twenty years. I sheepishly took my place in line and then knelt at the altar, waiting my turn. I had tears flowing down my face as Reverend Beacon gave me communion; then, the server offered me the chalice of wine. It was a very gratifying moment in my life; I again felt one with God. I did, however, beat myself up for being so ignorant all these years, blaming God because I did not have the proper relationship with him. It turns out that God was there all along; I just failed to realize it.

As with every new family, there is a feeling-out period, and ours with St. Andrew's was a quick and easy one. Heather, Travis, Tyler, and I attend as a family every week the boys are home and as a couple when they are with their dad. We look forward to going to choir practice each week as well. I am happy to have been blessed with this new family and feel very privileged to be a part of it and church again.

I don't want to come across as a bible thumper because I'm not, but I do realize the importance of spirituality in fighting bipolar disorder. It helps to have God with you to give you that guidance and push you need on the days that are tough and seem unbearable. The thing I like about church is the coming together of community at God's table. I am a comedian and like making people laugh even in church; then, you also have the opportunity of talking and laughing. There is something about having people together to share the word of God and mingling afterwards. There is no stress, no workplace politics, or all the day-to-day crap we have to put up with. Church is like a refuge for me. I have always found sanctuary there.

St. Andrew's has another special meaning for me, and that is that St. Andrew is the patron saint of Scotland. All through my romance and courtship with Heather, there have been signs and signals of what is to come. Our relationship has come a long way since we first met, and with Heather being determined, it has grown spiritually as well. This is my fairy tale relationship, especially with how it started. The icing on the cake will be our wedding at St. Andrew's in May of 2008. I realize that a building does not make a church; it's the people that make the church, a gathering of the people, and at St. Andrew's, it's a gathering of family.

Reverend Beacon (Joanne) invited Heather and me over to her home for dinner one Saturday night a few weeks after we started going to St. Andrew's. She was very open, and we shared lots of stories about everything and anything, even a little about God, too. We had Joanne over to our place a few weeks after and enjoyed her company again. Joanne is excellent at what she does, and we have developed a close relationship with her both as a reverend and friend. She is a genuine person with a great compassion for people who doesn't mind showing her emotions and is a credit to her faith. Joanne will marry Heather and me in May, and I look forward to her celebrating the Eucharist, which will be a first for me, even though I have been married three times before.

I have been preparing for this service for a few months, writing hymns and composing music. It's been fun and rewarding. I am not worried about the reception, only about the church. I don't care if we eat hotdogs and Kraft dinner at the reception, but I'm sure Heather won't go for that. We have moved our wedding date three times now, and after living as a couple for two years, and really going through a lot of rough times, I think we are ready to love each other as husband and wife.

Travis and Tyler are both being baptized this Sunday, and they are excited about the whole ordeal. For two kids, they have really taken a liking to going to church. We were out getting new clothes for them today, and they were happy as they looked and felt like men. I get a kick out of that, as I can relate to how they feel. I was having a shave a few weeks ago, and the bathroom door was open; the boys saw me shaving, and the next thing I knew, they had their fake razors and shaving cream out. The three of us had a few laughs, and again, they felt like men, as we all shaved around the sink. I will be delighted on Sunday as I will be Travis and Tyler's godfather; I look forward to teaching them many lessons about God and life. These two young men of eight years of age have made me laugh and taught me an awful lot about myself in the two and a half years we have been associated. They are like sons to me now, and I treat them as such. Heather figures I've created replicas of Dave, but I know I have put my influence into making them responsible and respectable young men. I am very proud of them and hope they continue this path they have chosen.

My faith in God was developed when I was born, as I was baptized a week after. I have always had a strong Catholic upbringing and always have had God on my shoulder. I believe in faith and that every person can make a difference, that life is what you make it, and, of course, to live for today, as you may not be here tomorrow. God has been good to me, giving me the strength to deal with bipolar disorder and enabling me to cope with life in a positive manner, even though there are days I definitely want to give up. It has been good for me to have God back in my life; it is certainly rewarding to have my beliefs come full circle.

We were disappointed a few weeks ago with the announcement that Reverend Beacon was leaving our parish. She is off to Niagara in Ontario. She explained to me personally that she had a hard decision to make and chose Niagara. I have nothing but the utmost respect for Joanne; she is a very funny person and I could get her going really easily. Our family will miss her immensely. I will miss her sermons and laugh. All the best, my friend, now go and teach the word of the Lord to Niagara. Don't be embarrassed when we show up there one of these years for a visit.

Joanne's last day was Sunday, January 27, 2008. Heather was confirmed, and I was received into the Anglican faith by Bishop Rodney Andrews. It was neat because Travis and Tyler were servers. I enjoyed meeting Bishop Rod; he is an exceptional person. Of course, I was teasing him that if we did the service the following week, he would look like St. Patrick, as the colors would change to green from the present burgundy. I had him laughing. He told me that he has high expectations for me to get involved in the vestry of the church. He was also very impressed with how the boys conducted themselves.

On the Thursday before the service, I went to choir practice, as I had written a song for Reverend Beacon. At the end of practice, I played it for her; she was very moved. Now, I normally don't do that, but I did on that night. I just played the music and handed out the words for everyone. I promised Joanne that I would put it on a disk with the help of Katie Nichol, the music director here at St. Andrew's.

I am very much looking forward to May 17, the date Heather and I finally get married; we will have both St. Andrew and St. Patrick with us in spirit on a very special date for us, marking the third anniversary of our first meeting. Heather was disappointed that Reverend Beacon could no longer marry us. The Irish and Scottish will be well represented; we will have bagpipes by Burt (Heather's dad), and for sure, I will play a few of my songs. We have no money, but are being very creative in how we are going to pull this off.

I am so lucky to have met Heather back on that long May weekend, as well as being very fortunate to now have her and her children in my life every day. I have enjoyed the first forty-five years of my life for the most part, and I'm looking forward to the next forty-five. Again, I thank you for purchasing this book; I enjoyed telling my story. I think Mrs. Leman would give me an A on this, too. Remember, folks, life is too short to hold grudges. Live life with your head held high and never be too proud to ask for help. Don't judge a person until you walk a mile in his or her shoes, even if they are bipolar shoes. We all deserve a chance. Work hard, live hard, play hard, and always be you.

When you are dealing with depression, try a couple of these tasks. Go for a short walk—no, not just to the fridge—a real walk, and have a chat with yourself. Ask yourself the hard questions about why you are depressed and set a plan of attack. I have found that listing weekly goals on a piece of paper and posting it where I can see it on a regular basis works for me. Get a couple of hobbies; for instance, I have my music, and I also enjoy writing. Hey, Mrs. Leman, did you hear that? I know she thinks I'm full of shit, as I detested writing in her class. Anyway, think positively and be around positive people.

I love to golf, and I am the first to admit that I suck at it. However, if I play with three really good players, my game comes up, and I make some great shots. Then, if I go with duffers like me, it's brutal.

I look at depression the same way: if I am the only one depressed and I am surrounded by happy people who are funny, I enjoy that a whole lot more than being around depressed people.

Everyone is different, but everyone should have a plan of attack. Be disciplined, stick to a routine, and take it easy on the booze. I used to drink about eight pints a day of Budweiser; I did that for many years, and now, I have a couple of Buds on a Friday after work; that's it.

Well, I haven't being keeping up with my commitment to myself, and that is writing my story. I have been keeping myself busy with work and family events. Today, I went outside at seven-thirty this morning to go to work, and the van wouldn't start. There are days that even the most trusted technology doesn't cut it when it's minus forty.

I always said after visiting Houston, Texas, for a leadership seminar that I would never complain about the cold again, as the heat was unbearable; well, I lied. It's so damn cold here right now that even the polar bears won't come out to play. This is insane. I wonder if cold weather makes a difference to one's mental health? Forty below is a little much, though I am hardy and Canadian, but the deep freeze is cruel and unusual punishment. Hell, frozen foods aren't this cold.

Then, to top it off, I got a postcard from Tim and Tammy from Mexico saying how nice it was there. The bad part for them is they got home two weeks ago, so they are in the freezer, too. Of course, I had to phone him and let him know I got his card with a few choice words thrown in for good measure. They enjoyed their holiday and are looking forward to going back next year. Tim has to travel to get away from the cold every year.

I'm looking forward to spending a few days in Edmonton for the family day long weekend. Tim and I will have a good few laughs. I am also looking forward to seeing Deirdre and Jacob. Deirdre must be showing by now; she is due in July with baby number two. She and Curtis have split up, so she will have her hands full with two children by herself. Angela bought her ticket to go and visit my mom. I was delighted for her when she told me; she never ceases to amaze me. I did not believe she would have the saving ability to pull that off, but she did. Angela is one determined person who also lives her dreams.

Since I have not been disciplined with my writing, a few things have happened. First, the family got a little bigger again, as Cody has moved back home. It was with some shock to both Heather and I that we saw how it was done. We had Cody for a visit, and when Heather took him home, he decided he didn't want to stay with his dad anymore. He has settled into school and is very happy with the decision he made. He has matured to the point that he knows where he belongs now. I have seen a great improvement in Cody's attitude, and it is a pleasure to have him back in our home. He is the type of young man that needs solid leadership in his life, with structure and proper direction. Cody and I have put the past behind us and embrace the future. This young man wants nothing more than to succeed in life while knowing he needs to be pushed.

I admire his courage and now understand that my psychiatrist, Dr. Mathews, was right when I discussed Cody in one of our appointments. I asked the doctor if Cody was showing traits of bipolar disorder and told him some of the problems I was having with his behavior and attitude. The doctor floored me with his answer that Cody loved me and was trying to convey that through his actions.

Travis and Tyler amazed me one day when they showed me their rock and shell collection. I spread them out on the bed and made two different patterns, one representing Horseshoe Canyon in Drumheller, Alberta, where we went for a weekend. The second represented every member of our family, and I was blown away that they were able to understand what I was thinking right down to every detail. It was truly remarkable that they could understand my concept that well.

Today is February 7, 2008. I have had a few stressful days and worked myself into a manic state. I have not slept more than four hours the last two nights combined; my brain is racing and I am exhausted. When I got up, I knew I was in trouble, so I decided I needed to inform my boss, Colin, about my situation. I was a little reluctant to tell him about bipolar disorder but decided it was the best course of action. He had no problem and appreciated the fact that I told him. I do not feel it will jeopardize my career. I am finishing this book now, as I want to concentrate on the opportunity Del-Air have given me to support my family. I thank each and every one of you that took the time to read my story. Let me tell you to never be scared to ask questions or to ask for help. You are the captain of your ship, so take charge of your life.

The following chapter is questions I asked myself. I hope this is useful to you all, and you never know, our paths may cross someday. Thanks again and God bless.

Dave O'Riordan

The Captain

I am the captain of my ship
that sails this sea of life.
I can navigate directions
and maintain a way of right.

This sea of life is often rough,
not for the faint of heart.
With all the dangers present,
being safe is just a start.

Now I'm halfway through the journey;
life has taken me by chance.
It's thrown all its fog and fury,
even all its gale-force storms.

The sea, it is my life.
It is the only thing I know.
I would like to see some calm again
before the journey's done.

Final Chapter

Tough Questions, Honest Answers

In this chapter, I would like to ask myself the tough questions while giving the honest answers; only a few people may dare to do this. I would like to shed some powerful light with my points of view on mental illness and with a real perspective on everyday life. I am entitled to my opinions with the liberty of expressing myself openly, and that is what I will attempt to pursue with this exercise. I have had many conversations with my friend Tim Johnson about a lot of issues over the years. We have a mutual respect for one another and can agree to disagree on certain aspects of life while maintaining our friendship. I will draw on Tim's knowledge as well as the lessons taught to me by my dad over my life.

The first question I have for myself is who my heroes were.

I have always put the men and women that serve and protect our world on the top of my list as my heroes. I have the utmost respect for all who have given their lives to enable me to have the freedom to express my opinions here in this book and every other aspect of my life. It is so easy to take for granted the hardships each and everyone of these people and their families have endured to protect our world and make it a better place for all of us. It was recently Remembrance Day here in Canada, and I was privileged to pay my respects to our lost veterans and troops serving around the world. I am lucky to have never had to experience war first hand in my time; I'm glad I didn't have to. Of course, the police departments and firefighters around the world also get my vote. Thank you to everyone who protects our world and who has given his or her life for the greater cause; thank you also to your families for their sacrifice. Of course, I don't just wait 'till Remembrance Day to appreciate their efforts; I do that every day.

Why did you decide to write *Bipolar Shoes*?

First off, I was tired of being rejected for employment opportunities where I live here in Humboldt. And in a dream, I had the idea to make this project happen. I wanted to take an illness that has cost me so much personally and financially and make it pay me back both financially and personally somehow, and that's how I decided to write *Bipolar Shoes*. I hope to return to school and obtain a degree so I can work with people that could benefit positively from my experience with bipolar disorder. There was a saying that went something like this: don't judge a man 'till you've walked a mile in his shoes. So here I have shared many miles with you—in my unique way, my bipolar shoes. I have been bothered by media reports, even with Bill O'Reilly, who I think is the best. The Oklahoma massacre was done by a person with a mental illness, and really, I felt it put a bad light over the rest of us who are good people suffering with mental illness. That fellow was a sick bastard that should have been committed well before this tragic event ever happened. As a person suffering from a mental illness, I felt discriminated against to a point, but realized that most people don't understand. I am an honest, hardworking man who loves life most of the time, and I wanted to share my story with everyone.

How did you learn to live a productive life after you were diagnosed with bipolar disorder, and what effect did bipolar disorder have on your attitude?

Believe it or not, my attitude was better when I found out I had a mental illness. I had to learn certain things all over again. Things like getting out of bed in the mornings were a chore, and now I had an excuse at thirty-three years of age. I always got myself up to go to work before I was diagnosed with this illness and I put myself back to doing just that. It was hard. I'm not exaggerating, but I was able to overcome my brain telling me one thing and my body telling me another. I fought with myself all the time and pushed hard on myself to be a productive person. I went to my doctor's appointments on a regular basis and took my meds when I was supposed to. Even now that I have run across tough times again, I keep myself busy doing things I like, such as writing poems or songs, and, of course, this book. I somehow have the imagination that I will be talking to a few people through this medium and want each and every one of you to realize that this whole book was typed with two fingers, and they are not the middle ones either, ha ha. Also, the spell check got a hell of a workout, and I got a whole new appreciation for education. It is hard to teach an old dog a new trick; however, I have, and I have enjoyed it at the same time, while still looking for work and lifting my leg.

Describe your feelings about moving from Ireland to Canada.

You can take the boy out of Ireland, but you can't take Ireland out of the boy. That is the best way I can describe it with no disrespect to Canada, which is now home to me and has been for thirty-three years. It was a struggle for me when I was a kid, as I was always torn between both countries. I guess if I was to explain it, I could see how my children felt going through divorce, with Ireland being my dad and Canada being my mom. It was no doubt hard as I didn't see Dad for a lot of years and always wondered how he was doing.

When you had your major breakdown, you referred to feeling the ultimate high; were you on drugs when you had your breakdown?

Hey, come here to me now! You're a cheeky bastard for asking me a question like that. The answer is I was not on drugs, nor have I ever been, for that matter, except for smoking pot on occasion, and yes, I did inhale. I was always afraid of trying hard drugs because of my addictive nature and the fact that my dad would have kicked the shit out of me. Even pot I didn't really like, as it would hit me hard, and I always felt as if I would lose control. I really didn't like that feeling a whole lot.

In this book, you made mention of being a pig and sleeping with a lot of women; how many did you sleep with?

You can go and feck yourself. I made mention of that fact because it is one of the traits of bipolar illness, you gobshite; it is classified information, for our knowledge only, right? Right, that's you sorted.

You have not made a lot of mention of friends in this book; is there any reason for that?

Yes, in my life, I have had many acquaintances, but not a whole lot of true friends that I would die for, if you know what I mean. Tim is my brother, more than my friend; I would go in the trenches for him always. I do love Tim and his family; they are my family.

I have also had the pleasure of getting acquainted with Tim's son Lee in the last couple of years. Tim and I had talked many times about Lee and his brother, Kyle, when we were single, and now Lee is back in Tim's life in a big way, as he is working with Tim every day. He also sees Kyle on occasion. Kyle is involved in the music business; he is a tremendous guitar player and writes amazing songs. I first met Kyle on St. Patrick's Day in 2005 and thought this kid was full of shit about the music stuff. After listening to his band's CD, I think the sky is the limit, pure talent.

Another friend of mine that I would go to the trenches for is Robert Elson. I worked with Robert a long time ago in McDonald's; he was best man for my first wedding, and I was his best man at both of his weddings. He is Angela's godfather and always has been a good friend to the family. Robert and I don't get together very often anymore, but we can count on each other when the need arises. He was very helpful during my dad's funeral. As with Tim, Robert and I have been there for each other through bad and good.

Graham Anderson is the last in my group of true friends; we enjoyed playing music together. Graham is an excellent guitar player; we drank beer and played tunes for hours at a time and always had a laugh. He was best man at my wedding to Corinne, and I was a groomsman at his wedding. We have lost touch in the last few years; maybe I will have to track him down and catch up on the news.

How important do you feel counselling is to maintaining your mental health?

I feel that it is very important for me to have an outlet that can somewhat relate to what I go through. I see my counsellor, Jen, once every two weeks and have a good feeling every time I walk out of her office. Counsellors can be a huge impact on your mental wellness, but you have to commit to being honest with yourself first before it can ever pay dividends to you. What I mean is don't sugar coat the facts to try to look good, because it doesn't work. I would have the same advice for people seeking couple's counselling: be honest; if you can't, then you shouldn't be there, because in my opinion, you're wasting your time. Let's face it: nobody likes to be kicked in the ass and told they are doing something wrong, but a counsellor's task is to get you on the right track and thinking positively about yourself. They are there to be an important part of your mental health team along with your doctors and family.

Do you suffer any side effects from medications that you take?

Yes, I do. As with a lot of medications, there are potential side effects. I have back and joint issues, along with a side effect involving depression and sleep problems, along with dry mouth with the pill Soritane, which I take for my skin disorder, Darier's; that can become very bothersome at times. I am dammed if I do and damned if I don't. With the lithium, it adds to dry mouth, is hard on my teeth, and I get tremors when I'm really tired or extremely agitated. I have to be very careful because the medication I take for my skin sets off bipolar disorder, and medication I have tried for bipolar disorder sets off my skin. I have a hard time balancing everything out. My main focus is the bipolar disorder, with the skin being secondary. I have learned to live with the discomfort.

You stated earlier that you knew something was wrong before you had your breakdown; why did you not get help then?

Excellent question: like most young people, I kept to myself, didn't share my thoughts with anyone, really. I always questioned myself but thought what was going on with me was normal. Remember, I only went to school for half of grade ten because the family moved back to Ireland, and I never did return to school when we came back. I threw myself into the adult world at a young age because I was bored at school and found it hard to sit in class for a prolonged period of time. I have always been a strong person, and at a young age, I did believe I was invincible, until I had the breakdown. It's easy to say after the fact that I should have gotten help, but really, that's just hindsight. I had no way of knowing what was wrong with me.

Describe how you felt being committed to a mental hospital for a month.

This is a really hard question for me to answer. First, I didn't feel anything. I was like a zombie. I was at peace with myself, feeling I was God while being strapped to a bed. Then, as time went on, I felt embarrassed and ashamed that I was in this place. I felt I was better and wanted to get the hell out of there. How could my business succeed if I was locked up? It took me about three days to understand that this was not a nightmare; this was real, and then I was scared—a scared feeling that I would describe as the fear that for the first time in my life, I had no control over anything. I learned to relax, not worry, and take care of myself. I had to keep myself busy, and I did; however, I was getting pissed off at being confined. The real world seemed so far away. I will say one thing: the nurses at the hospital were superb. I was treated better than most of the other patients, in my opinion, because I was a business owner and had a bit of money.

I remember being extremely agitated one day and blowing a gasket on the doctors because they would not let me go home. I was there for only two weeks. I had some very colorful language and went on a rant for about an hour. I was so pissed off that I gave everyone in the smoke room a pack of cigarettes because I felt sorry for them. Quite a few of these people would empty out the ashtrays and roll the butts; they had no money, and now I was really pissed off. I was yelling at the doctors and giving them shit. Of course, the doctor called my dad and told him what was going on. Dad came down and we talked I was still fuming, but now I was pissed off at the system. Listen to this for a second: in talking to a nurse, he informed me that most of the patients would never get out of the hospital. He also told me that convicts get better perks than mental health patients, like free cigarettes. Now I was seeing red. These poor people did nothing wrong, yet our system treats convicts better; what the f--- is going on here? I said to myself.

I met some very interesting people while in the hospital. One comes to mind. He was known as "One Eye." He had been in the hospital for twenty-seven years and was now being released to a halfway house in Edmonton. I felt sorry for this man, as he did not want to be released; he was probably in his sixties and very scared of what life had in store for him. I again used my inner strength and realized that here I was, trying to get out, and this poor bastard was trying to stay in. My problems did not seem so big then, as I knew I was getting out soon. All in all, my experience being committed to a mental hospital was not one I would recommend to anyone; however, that said, it has made a huge impact on my life. I never forget the people I met and do think of them often. It was a month out of my life that changed me forever—in a positive way, I might add, as I never want to go back as a patient again.

What was the hardest thing for you to deal with after your breakdown?

There were several things I had to deal with. First and foremost, I had to re-evaluate my capabilities and myself. I had to get over the shame I felt and what I had done in my past by letting go and realizing that my life was now really just starting, so I wiped the slate clean. I had to learn not to beat up on myself so much even though, at times, I still do.

However, the hardest thing to do was learn to live with bipolar disorder while understanding that I am a person who is not disabled, even though some days it is so hard to function properly. I was also concerned about how my family and friends would treat me, and I'm happy to say they did not treat me any differently. I remember a friend, Steve Dunlop, telling me one night when we were out with the gang that he wouldn't let me take a cab. This was a huge icebreaker, and the gang of us laughed.

The hardest thing was regaining my confidence and understanding that I had an illness that I had to manage properly; frankly, this scared the shit out of me. As I have stated many times, don't be afraid to get help and use the resources available to you. There are great Web sites and communities on Facebook where you can interact with people who deal with this illness.

So with all your years of living with bipolar disorder, what has been your greatest accomplishment?

That would be waking up every morning with a positive attitude, ready to appreciate life for the little things. There was a day when I wanted to be a millionaire along with being famous, but really, now I know that I am happy where I am in life, and it's not all about money. You can always make more money; however, it's hard to get back what you lost.

With accomplishment comes failure. I believe that I let my children down by not understanding their needs. I am not saying I was a bad father, but I believe I am a better father figure now to Heather's children than I ever was to my daughters. By the way, I spent some time with my daughter, Cassie, when I was in Edmonton recently; to be honest; I made arrangements to meet her in the food court of a shopping center. I was sitting there, watching people, when out of the blue, this young lady sat at my table. It is normal for people to plonk themselves down when it is really busy.

I took a second look and realized it was Cassie. I didn't recognize her; she now has long black hair and is skinny. She looked really good, and I was so glad to finally see her after not seeing her for two years. We only spent an hour together, but it was an accomplishment. I am so lucky to have three wonderful daughters that I have helped shape into terrific people that I am very proud of. Life for me has always been about my children; they have been my strength and inspiration, as well as my reason to persevere through this journey of life. They are, for sure, my biggest accomplishment. I had a very adult conversation with Cassie that afternoon in the mall. I opened the door for her to talk about her problems and gave her some frank advice, and that was to be herself. She looks terrific, I am glad she agreed to meet me.

My most recent accomplishment is writing this book. I am proud of the work I have achieved with *Bipolar Shoes*. It's pretty good for a guy typing with two fingers and a grade nine education. I know it will help some people by telling the story of an ordinary man who has lead an extraordinary life.

What are your favourite movies, songs, and books?

I really like the Shrek movies. I find them funny with an appeal to children as well as adults. I can watch them over and over.

Music is a passion that I have always had, and every song tells a story. I like a wide assortment of music and artists, from rock to country, some folk, and alternative. One of my favorite songs is by Simple Plan, called "Perfect." I was on Angela's case about stuff when she lived with me. She sent me an email with that song, and I got the message. I then sent her back with the song "Teach Your Children Well" by Crosby, Stills, and Nash.

I am not a really big reader, but I really enjoyed *The Five People You Meet in Heaven* and *Tuesdays with Morrie* by author Mitch Albom.

For television, I like *House*, as he's a cranky bastard just like me. *The O'Reilly Factor* gets watched every night. I also enjoy watching the UFC on Spike TV.

I have invited my family to partake in this question-and-answer session. Heather has asked the following questions.

On average, about how often would you say that you "cycle," and how long does each "cycle" last?

Well, my last cycle was in the fall. I needed a pack of smokes, and it lasted about six minutes from the time I left the house till I got back. It was not even enough time to get the seat warm on the bicycle. Really, that is a very hard question. I have bipolar 1 and do experience rapid cycling, but to actually put a time frame together is unrealistic.

What I mean by that is there are many factors involved. Being tagged with bipolar disorder has its curses, and for me, this is one. You see, I am just an average person until someone finds out I'm bipolar, and then, the rules change. I have experienced both mania and depression in the same day. I have done this project also in both states. The longest I have experienced depression is six to eight months, and there were some good days in there, too. The longest mania was about two weeks; that was physically draining. It is much easier for me to deal with cycles like training for a bike race. The more you train, the more you know what to expect from your body. I have been training with bipolar disorder now for many years and know how to get help if, say, I injure myself training.

Would it be realistic to call the period of time between normal and irrational behavior "cycling"? And each episode of behaviors, beginning with racing thoughts, no sleep, lack of appetite, irritability to the point of depression—how long would you say each episode typically lasts?

Well, Heather, I don't know; I don't think it would be realistic, as it's normal. Please tell me this: what is normal? I think you are confusing certain issues; racing thoughts and no sleep are signs of mania. I, for one, have a bad habit of thinking out loud and jumping from topic to topic. Sometimes, the way I express myself is confused with irrational behavior. It is hard enough to live with this illness, then to feel as if your every move is analyzed. I am a person who, I am happy to say, is unique in my approach to life, and that, along with being bipolar, is who I am. Yes, I get irritable, but just because I get irritable doesn't make me depressed or manic. On this question, you should probably ask a doctor for some insight, as I am a little confused about what you are really asking. I'm thinking maybe you mean to ask why I eat, sleep, and drink a project to the point where it consumes me, which is irrational. That is not the illness; that is just my trait and commitment to myself as I am extremely focused on tasks I do.

I would imagine that a person would be both emotionally and physically drained, as well as perhaps have stress headaches during a manic episode; do you have pain during this time?

It depends on what level I'm at. Let's say I can't sleep; then, yes, I have headaches. I know that I need to sleep and work myself into a panic about how I'm going to function the next day. For example, I have had a hard time sleeping the last few nights because I have a lot on my plate with this project, as well as preparing to move house at the end of March. Then, our wedding in May plus the everyday tasks and responsibilities of work are starting to overwhelm me. I cannot do a good job on everything if I load myself up so much. My main function now is work, and I realize that I have to cut some of my workload, as it is emotionally and physically draining.

I often think that you only think of yourself during these times, as this is when my feelings get hurt a lot. Do you think of other people's feelings or just focus on what you're dealing with?

These are tough questions, so here is my honest answer. If I only thought of myself, my life would have been over a long time ago. I hurt your feelings because what is important to you at the time is unimportant to me. I am only worried about getting better as fast as possible. That's not right, I know, but it is honest.

When I am depressed, I don't care about anything. I have to work through my emotions. I don't want to be bothered with menial things, even though it's important to you. In a lot of cases, I am trying to deal with just functioning normally; the biggest problem is that everything I say and do is under the microscope with you. I convey the message to you that I'm not doing well mentally, and then you start crying; that does not help my situation, and honestly, it makes it worse. I don't think of myself enough. I think about everyone else first.

I have said many times already that life is a challenge for everyone; no matter what a person has, he or she always wants more. I just want to be happy, and I am with you. I would appreciate you understanding that and not holding on to everything I say, even if it was two years ago. Heather, I am a person who lives with a mental illness, and I know what's going on most of the time. In our relationship, I have made mention of bailing, and you were able to notice a trend from my past that rears its ugly head. When I had had enough, you were smart enough to point that out to me.

Do you think you could hurt yourself or others?

Yes, I think that is possible, and no, I don't think I would. The only time I didn't recall my actions was the night I had the breakdown where I was committed for being a danger to others and myself. I am a passive person until provoked, and then, I'm a pit bull with very aggressive tendencies. I have mellowed in the last ten years and learned to control my aggression by not getting involved in situations where I get provoked. In all my years, I have never started an altercation, but I have finished quite a few. I have not hit a person in over twelve years; the last fight was against two fellows, and I got my ass kicked and decided I should retire and keep my good looks. I have not come out of retirement and don't plan to anytime soon.

Now, I'm always told that people with bipolar disorder always want the last word; well, that is not the case in this instance. Deirdre and Heather both wrote about how mental illness affected their lives, and I thank them for their input. Nobody has to tell me how hard it is to live with someone who has bipolar disorder or any other mental illness, for that matter. It is hard on everyone, sometimes devastating. I am more aware of my actions now; however, sometimes I still say hurtful things to people. Please do give me your feedback by checking out http://daveoriordan.com. I welcome your comments. Thank you for walking a mile in my shoes. God bless and all the best. Take care, Dave

Deirdre gave me the following letter with her opinions and comments; it goes like this.

Depression has always been a part of my life. I myself have never been affected with it, but it indirectly has always affected me. Growing up, my life wasn't easy, but in life, whose ever is? My father was always the person who talked about big things and never really lived up to them. I felt always that I was never good enough for him and that I was always competing for his affection.

Dad was always a confusing person: one minute you're buddy-buddy, and then, like a light switch, there was an alternate ego. I always fought hard for his affection but never knew that my hard work was dissipating over his illness. I remember one moment in particular when I was turning twelve; it was my birthday, and Dad told me that it had been a rough year and that he couldn't get me a gift, which wasn't a concern for me; I was just happy he was there. We had thrown a double birthday party for my little sister and I; it was great until he brought out all the gifts for her and told me that she was too young to understand and that it was nothing personal.

I was hurt and angry, but I always tried to stick it out because I liked the dad he sometimes was. I never tried to understand what bipolar disorder was. I never really cared. I just tried to distance myself from whatever it was to avoid getting hurt, and that always seemed to work best. As I got older, I always tried to put the past behind me and move forward with my life.

I travelled with the carnival and tried to experience many different things in life and many new people. When it was time to head back home, I always dreaded whatever dramas were headed my way. I tried to brush it off and work it out. When I got home, I moved in with my sister and actually started to see more of my dad. It was great; we would hang out, have dinner, play music, and sing.

I finally started to feel as if I had my father back. When I found out I was pregnant, I even told my father before my mom, which was something I had never done.

Much to the dismay of everyone else, I was growing closer with my dad, and we were building that bond again. Little did I know that right around the corner heartbreak was about to strike again. I was working at my pub, Sherlock Holmes, as I did every night, when my dad came in. It was nice to talk to him again. Much like what happened every other night, Dad got a little carried away with how much he had to drink. I offered to drive him home because he had already gotten charged with a couple of impaired driving offences, and I didn't mind driving him home.

We grabbed some coffee and headed back to his place, where I wanted to give him his surprise: a couple of INXS tickets, a band we both like. We got talking and as usual, Dad went on a rant about how my life wasn't going well and I shouldn't do things the way I was. He knew full well that I don't take crap from anyone or listen to advice coming from someone who is sitting in my position and should be the last to judge. I told him how I felt about it, and he snapped.

Dad knows when he has reached that breaking point, but it's as if he has no control and thrives on whatever consequences it has. I didn't talk to Dad for several months after that. He moved away to Saskatchewan to be with Heather (his fiancé) and her boys. He never made an effort to contact me, and neither did I contact him. We always kind of kept in touch through a third party, so when my son was born in early October, it didn't surprise me that Dad felt he had to be a part of my life again. This time, I wasn't having it; not only did I have the confrontations with my dad on my mind; I had my own relationship that would soon be finding its way down the same path. My boyfriend, Curtis, suffers from depression also, and it was hard to learn that I was so in love with someone who was so much like my dad. Unlike my father, Curtis had an addiction to marijuana, which, like Dad's drinking, affected his depression. He had a hard time keeping a job and getting out of bed. At this time, I found myself being a motivator and trying to stay positive, because just as I loved my father, I loved Curtis and wanted him to change. The hardest part about this was that I found myself trying so hard to help him that I forgot about myself. I found myself being brought down, too.

It was at this point that I felt as if I needed to do my homework so I could see what I was getting into and learned the best thing I needed to know, which is that you can't help someone who doesn't want to help himself or herself. This was an extremely hard lesson to learn. Why can you love someone so much that you devote all your power to helping him or her get better, however, he or she still doesn't want to help him- or herself?

Finally, things were turning for the good in my relationship. Curtis got a great job and was taking his meds every day; he was the most amazing person ever. I felt as if I had done it and I was ready for anything. My dad had decided he was coming to Edmonton for a week, and I knew he had no money, so I offered to let him stay with me (I was unstoppable). We had a heartfelt talk that was cut short when he told me that the reason he was never there for me was because I was strong and I could take care of myself, whereas my other two sisters needed him ... Was this supposed to be a compliment? How is it that because someone is strong he or she doesn't need a father in his or her life? Was he kidding? What a buzz kill it was; at this point, I realized that you really can't change someone.

I have avoided phone calls from my dad because I don't want to hear his stories and because I don't want to let him in my life to hurt me again. Does this make me smart? Or intolerant of someone else's faults? As I have realized in my relationship with my father and now my relationship with Curtis, I have tried; I have made a grave effort. There is only so much that one person can do before it's too much. There is only so much hope that one person can bring before you, too, join the circle of high hopes and letdowns.

Having these depressions in my life has really shown me that it's not that these people can't love you; it's that they need to find strength from within themselves to pick up the pieces to rebuild their lives, and what you do can help or hurt that cycle.

I only hope that what I have done now by keeping myself back from Dad and just letting things be, and by letting Curtis go so that he can find himself without having the pressures of what I want for my life bring him down is the best thing possible for both these relationships to work out in the end.

Deirdre O'Riordan, 2008

How has living with a person with bipolar disorder affected me? What a tough question; I mean, why not just ask me why the sky is blue?

I have told Dave on several occasions that I love the person but I hate the illness. I hate what it does to Dave, how it makes him treat my children and me, but mostly how it makes him beat himself up. This illness, bipolar disorder, is like living with Dr. Jekyll and Mr. Hyde ... I wonder if manic depression is where the concept for Dr. Jekyll and Mr. Hyde came from in the first place. Waking in the morning and not knowing what to expect, if it's going to be a good day or if we have to walk on eggshells, is the worst part of this illness. To be totally honest, if I hadn't fallen in love with Dave before I actually saw what the illness did to him, he would not be in my life. I would not have had the patience to deal with more issues, chaos, and drama in my life than I already had.

I believe that everything happens for a reason and that fate brought Dave and me together. The way that we met, learning about each other over the Internet and phone, becoming friends and learning about each other before we met in person, was a big plus. Dave told me about his bipolar disorder and Darier's disease before we met in person. I think it was his way of giving me advance notice of a way out if I wanted it. It was too late by that time. He had already stolen my heart.

I spent time learning about bipolar disorder and watching Dave's mood cycles. I have learned when to bite my tongue, clench my fists, and hang on for the spin of torment before he crashes from manic state into depression. Bipolar disorder is a family affair; if you don't know what to expect or how to manage it, it will be disastrous to any relationship. Dave does a great job of managing his moods, making sure he takes his medications. He is very well in tune with himself and is not afraid to ask for help when he needs it. I think this is the biggest obstacle any person with mental illness needs to learn. My advice to any of you out there reading this book and living with a person with bipolar disorder is to learn his or her mood cycles and learn what best works for you to avoid his or her triggers. Also, let the person know what behaviors you will not tolerate. For example, I will not put up with Dave's willingness to run away whenever things get tough, and Dave knows it. He may feel like walking away from our relationship, but we have spent too long and sacrificed too much. I am too stubborn to let a pissy mood destroy everything we've worked so hard for. I am not going to let him walk away when his mental condition is not stable enough to make that big a decision.

The biggest ingredient that was missing in Dave's past relationships, in my opinion, is education, both on Dave's part and on the part of his wife (at the time). If Dave had lived with his wives before marrying them, and if they had become familiar with his moods and about how bipolar disorder affected them, their relationships would have been more tolerable and understanding.

Don't get me wrong; bipolar disorder is not a curse, and it's not a constant struggle of frustration, even though the first thing a person tends to do is cringe when they hear "bipolar." I think this is because so many people focus on the negative. It doesn't help that people don't understand and therefore, the ones who are affected are labeled as being maniacs, crazy, or dangerous. After all, who has ever heard of the press informing the public that some wonderful person is "affected" with a mental illness? Why can't a person be "gifted" with bipolar disorder? After all, those who are in a manic state are gifted with wonderful creativity. There are some gifted authors and artists out there who have this gift. It is a shame that we only hear about the negative news giving details about mental illness playing a role in some tragedies. Science and medicine have come a long way; one can only hope that the human race can also come out of the dark ages, learn about mental illness without the negative stigma attached, and love each individual for who he or she is, not for what he or she may or may not be afflicted with.

I love Dave for the person he is, how he brings the best out in my children and me. We connect on an amazing level and are in tune with each other. We have a very strong bond, and our relationship, I believe, will last our lifetimes, because we are educated about bipolar disorder and all its gifted glory.

Dave has a lot of great qualities. One of his greatest qualities is his honesty; he is brutally honest. I have learned not to ask how I look anymore; I would rather wait to see if I get a compliment or not.

When I first told Dave that I had four boys, I told him that I was not looking for a father for them, as they already had one; I was looking for a companion for myself. I did not realize at the time that Dave would come into my children's lives and show them what men were made of. I was always afraid as a single parent of boys that I would raise mama's boys. Dave assured me that my boys were just that, typical boys that needed some direction. Dave is the best thing that could have ever happened to those four boys of mine. They gained a positive male influence in their daily lives, a confidant and best friend. Dave knows things about my children that I don't. He has a way with joking, laughing, and teaching them that is phenomenal. I once read a little poem that read, "Anyone can be a father; it takes someone special to be a dad." I believe this to be true.

I joked with Dave that he should write a book on raising children because he has a magical way of relating to kids. Who knows? Maybe that will be his next project.

Heather Morrow, soon to be O'Riordan, 2008

Okay, the Last Word

The date is now October 3, 2008; it has been many months since I have done anything on this project. With the financial help of my mother, Pat, I am getting this project published. It will be done in 2009, so another goal is achieved, thanks to a lot of help from a lot of people. Please excuse me for grammar errors and spelling mistakes; editing was not in the budget. It's hard to drink Champagne on a beer budget, right Louie? I remember.

Heather and I achieved another goal by finally becoming husband and wife on May 17 in a very personal ceremony performed by Reverend Gordon Lines at St. Andrew's Church here in Humboldt. It was everything we had hoped for and more.

Deirdre gave birth to my second grandson, Kobe, on Father's Day, June 15, 2008. Jacob turned two today. Time does march on, and I am looking forward to spending time with Jacob and Kobe as a granddad.

Being one never to be left behind, Angela is going to tie the score in one shot. Sophia and Julia will be born in the next little while. I am told its identical twin girls she is having; she has no idea what she's in for. One is hard enough; it's going to be a lot of work for her and Alex. I am very proud of Angela, Deirdre, and Cassie; they are the main reason I am still alive today. Really, though, I am extremely proud of myself for being able to live with this mental illness and not be afraid to tell my story to the world. Bipolar disorder is part of my being, and I have learned to cope with the roller coaster rides it brings.

I do not use it as an excuse, and I push myself very hard for results. It is too easy to give in to the darkness of depression and lose all motivation to do anything. Some days, I am glad that I don't have lots of money, because I could guarantee you I would stay home from work when I am depressed. Being like I am financially, I can't afford to miss work. It works for me to get up and go, even though I don't feel like it. I am engaged in all sorts of activities at work that keep me occupied.

So here we are, on the Canadian Thanksgiving weekend, and boy, do I have a lot to be thankful for. My family started out as five in Canada back in 1974. Since that time, it has increased to a respectable number of twenty-five and a half, with the arrival of Sophia and Julia on the eighth of October, 2008.

I remember at my dad's funeral when Rob gave the eulogy, he said that Dad's favourite title in life was "Granddad," and that's where I am now. I am very thankful to have four grandchildren at the young age of forty-six. It certainly gives new inspiration and a new perspective to look at life. I am also grateful Angela and the girls are doing well and are now home with Alex.

I am thankful that my wife, Heather, is so understanding of what I go through and is always there for me, no matter what. I appreciate her and love her for her compassion and thoughtfulness. I even like her silly jokes. All in all, I am thankful for the wonderful family that I have. We may not see eye to eye on everything, but that's okay in my book. Everyone is entitled to his or her opinions, even if I don't agree with them, and at the end of the day, we are still family.

I have shed many tears writing this book. I have also laughed and have been embarrassed by the things I have done. I have learned that I'm human; I have learned that I can love. I have realized that I am a good person who does very well living with a mental illness. I am very much aware of my mental state and know when I am going to have issues. This did not just happen; it took years of experiencing to finally be able to see the signs, to understand what was going on.

Updating the Story

The date is now August 23rd, 2009 I have a couple of days before this book gets formatted and is launched. Authorhouse has promised to have the book available for my birthday September 17th and it will be my present to myself.

I lost my job on December 4th 2008 and Del-Air Systems went bankrupt soon after in March 2009. This was the first time I was ever fired from a job and I didn't like it. I sued for wrongful dismissal but got nowhere as they closed the business. It's been hard on my mental health not working and I hope that changes soon.

Just to let you know, I have come full circle. On July 21st I admitted myself into the hospital here in Humboldt. I was having problems sleeping, eating, and thinking clearly I was in a manic state. I was released from the hospital on the 23rd feeling better. I slept pretty well that night but I was very restless according to Heather. I had an appointment with Dr. Mathews set up for Friday the 24th in Saskatoon and I explained everything to him. He increased my dosage of Seroquel to 75mg and I was on my way I thought.

That night I had a hell of a time sleeping and was up several times I may have got 4 hours sleep. I had made a commitment to Heather that I would pick up Cody in Saskatoon as he was coming home from cadet camp. Heather had an engagement being a clown so I asked my mother-in-law Maggie to come with me to Saskatoon for company. Maggie had broken her foot a couple of weeks earlier so she had a cast on her foot. Heather and I helped her out to the van and Heather took Maggie's car. Everything seemed fine with me I was laughing and joking with Maggie. When we arrived in Saskatoon I felt a little out of sorts but took no notice of it. I missed the turn for the airport and got lost I remember pulling the van over giving Maggie a hug and telling her that I would shut up and she could give me directions to the Airport. I really don't remember getting there however I remember giving Cody a big hug and signing my name "Happy Day" where my signature was supposed to go.

I remember nothing after that, until we were halfway home and realized I wasn't driving. I sat there quiet in the van, trying to understand what the hell had happened. I noticed nobody was talking and everyone was in a sombre mood so I started talking. Pretty soon we were laughing and talking as nothing happened. We arrived back in Humboldt at about 5pm Heather was soon to arrive back at Maggie's. I am going to let Heather tell the rest of this story as it is very sketchy to me.

Signs – by Heather O'Riordan

I pulled around the corner and found Dave, Cody and my mom at the van. Dave was helping my mom from the van to her walker so she could get to her house, everything was fine, or so I thought. I went into the house where Dave had a strange smile on his face and a look of mischief in his eye and he kept saying "nobody believes me"; "nobody believes that I can change". I questioned him out of pure confusion and he just smiled. I was asking Cody about his trip and noticed that my mom and Cody both had a strange look of confusion, like they were hiding something from me. (You know that look when someone wants to tell you something but there is someone else present that you don't want to hear the conversation?) Naturally I asked what was going on when suddenly Dave jumped into the middle of the living room and yelled "yippee". I knew right there that Dave was manic and both Cody and mom had seen something they did not want to be a part of. Dave then ran outside jumping and "yipping". My mom's neighbour came home so Dave decided to give her a hug and made a comment about how she was going to live after all (she has cancer). He then climbed on to the back of my van and started to pound his fists on the roof. I told Dave to come with me; I thought he should go to the Hospital to get some help. Dave's reply was a slur of obscenities. I knew without a doubt that what he was experiencing was a psychotic break like the one he had told me about and written about so many years before. I warned Dave to get into the van or I would call 911.

Dave had told me long ago that if I was ever concerned about his mental health that I should call the police. I dialled 911 on my cell phone while trying to convince Dave to get into the van. I explained to the operator that I needed an ambulance and police; I was not sure of what Dave was capable of doing to himself or others.

I think you could probably imagine the look on the paramedics and police officers faces as they drove up to find a clown comforting a cadet (in uniform). While a middle-aged man was jumping around "yipping" and talking about how people don't believe how he can change. It was a sight. Anyway, Dave told the paramedics and police that he was on his way to Ireland for two years with his buddy Tim and his mom, he was not going to the hospital. Dave didn't know where he was, where he lived or his name. He was getting agitated with all the questions and threw his wallet; and change from his pocket and his glasses into the street. I had him arrested to get him into the ambulance, by that time he asked if he could get a ride to the hospital but first he wanted to stop at the bar to drink some beer.

I arrived at the hospital (after changing out of my clowning gear) Dave did not recognize me, his eyes were glazed over and he was confused. I went into the examination room three times before the drugs that were administered took effect enough for him to recognize me and ask why he was in the hospital and why he was handcuffed. I spoke to the police, paramedics and doctor, and agreed that he should be admitted to a facility to better cope with mental illness. The police took our home address in case of any future incidents that may occur and explained that the "arrest" would not show up on any record; it was only a tactic to get Dave to the Hospital safely. The doctor on duty stayed out of the room as much as possible as Dave had built a rapport with one of the paramedics and this particular doctor knew that his presence would only aggravate Dave further.

I had no idea this was going to happen. He was fine when I left him with my mom to go to Saskatoon earlier in the day. Apparently after picking Cody up at the airport, Dave drove through the city at high speeds into areas that he didn't know, heading out of town in a direction that we never travel. My mom had to yell to get him to pull the van over and let her drive. She said that he had a glazed look over his eyes, and was "out of it." My mom had to tell him step-by-step how to get out of the van and into the passenger seat.

Dave was transferred to the Royal University Hospital in Saskatoon. The one hour drive there seemed to take forever as my mind would wander back to his last "episode" when Dave wound up in Ponoka for a month. I hoped he wouldn't have the same long stay in Saskatoon. I also worried if he were to get violent in the ambulance. I spoke to what seemed like an endless stream of doctors telling the story over and over about the lack of sleep, mounting stress and general health complaints Dave had complained about for the past couple of months. I told of his "adventures" with his previous psychotic break and how he was diagnosed as being Bipolar. I explained how the day's events played out first for my mom then for myself. Finally, after what seemed like an eternity I was able to see my husband. He looked so peaceful curled up on a bed in a guarded room. It reminded me of a jail cell that one would see in a movie. Dave looked up at me, told me he was so tired and asked me to lay down with him. He was like a frightened child in an unfamiliar place.

Dave was then admitted to the psychiatric ward where he stayed for a week. I felt guilty for having to call 911, and have him arrested and sent to Saskatoon, but I know that I did the right thing I got the help that was needed. Cody came to the Hospital with me to visit Dave a few days later and he is alright with what happened. I'm just thankful that Dave told me long ago that if I was ever concerned to call the police. I'm glad I saw the signs and they didn't get any worse before he got the help he needed. Bipolar disorder is like Dr. Jekyll & Mr. Hyde. I hate the illness but I love the man.

Heather O'Riordan

Okay so there it is in a nut shell I had another major breakdown. I know that again, I was thinking I was God at that time. Why this happened again to me I have no idea however I was able to use my past experience to make this one a bit easier to handle. Somewhere in the middle of this ordeal I realized something was dreadfully wrong. Why was I was telling a clown to eff off and calling her a bitch. After all the clown was my wife, my best friend and a person I admire. Something clicked in my head and I started cooperating.

Just to set the record straight I was not arrested or charged with anything the handcuffs were for the safety of the police and ambulance personnel as I was unpredictable. I cooperated the whole time. I had a sombre ride in the ambulance from the hospital in Humboldt to the Royal University Hospital in Saskatoon. I was restrained with bandages on my wrists that were tied to the stretcher. The medications they had given me in Humboldt were now in effect. The whole day seemed like a bad dream to me as I replayed the events I remembered and beat myself up for what had happened. I had made arrangements so I thought to have my friend Tim and his family accompany me on a trip to Ireland with Heather and the kids. My mom and my daughters were also part of my plan. You see I believed I was God, but again I was wrong my dad again functioned into my mind and he was God. I always remember my dad telling me to take my time and not rush into making decisions. I had picked the people that mean the most to me to help me make the right decisions. I have always rushed decisions that's why the two year trip was planned it was to give me time to think. "The nobody believes in me" quote I used was when I thought I was Jesus.

As it turned out it didn't matter because the same as the first time I had a breakdown I came crashing down to reality. I realized I wasn't God and to be honest I was disappointed it was like thinking you won the lottery and someone took it away from you except it had now happened to me twice.

I was admitted to the hospital after a battery of questions. This time I was a voluntary patient rather than being committed. I credit Heather with this as she followed what I had told her in regards to getting help if I was out of sorts. When I was taken to my room Heather accompanied me I gave her a hug a thanked her for everything.

I slept that night like a baby, when I woke up I felt much better. This time I wasn't looking for answers and I felt no guilt or shame. I was laughing at the thought of me jumping up and down saying yippee. I didn't feel the need to punish myself by trying to figure out what happened. I accepted it and knew I was in the right place to get better.

While I was in the hospital I thought about this book and I came to the understanding again that everything happens for a reason. You see I was going to market my book and sell as many copies as I could. It was in the hospital going through another recovery that I really understood for the first time what this book means to me, and how much impact it could have on other people. I was able to combat all my fears and just concentrate on me getting well. I was able to attain this by taking my own advice and using my knowledge from before that I shared in Bipolar Shoes.

There will be some people who think this book is good and helpful to them, and there will be others who think it's shite that's okay with me. The only reason I wrote Bipolar Shoes is to help people understand mental illness by using my perspective. I am glad now that I had so many problems getting this book published and that I made the decision to include this update story. As I said everything happens for a reason. I am feeling great since being released from the hospital. My medications were adjusted again and everything seems to be on the right track.

Breakdowns can't always be predicted as I have just explained and it's an awful feeling when you come down especially when you feel so wonderful when you believe your God. I have attained world peace twice and everyone got along with no violence or hardships. When I have been in that state of mind I have only had one outcome and that is peace and happiness for everybody. It truly is a wonderful feeling when in your mind you are surrounding yourself with the people who mean everything to you but it is a huge crash when you come back to reality. I was a little more prepared this time and again I had excellent care from the staff of the hospital.

With this breakdown I have learned that Heather is a special person sent from God to help me cope with life as well as bipolar disorder she has been terrific. Since all this happened I have not spoke to her mother Maggie as she has nothing nice to say about me. That's okay, why should she be different than most other people who can't deal with mental illness. This is where the stigma starts. She had concerns with me being home with the boys alone and what happens if I have another episode as she puts it.

What I want to know is why she threw me under the bus because of this? I wrote Maggie a note when I was in the hospital that thanked her for dealing with the situation. She didn't receive the note as I asked Heather not to give it to her because of her reaction towards me. She has not phoned me to see how I'm doing and I'm fine with that too, however I am disappointed. I will let the situation have a little more time before I approach her. In going through this whole ordeal I really realized who was the most important people to me.

While I was in the hospital Heather wrote me a poem it goes like this;

I wish I had my magic wand
to cast a magic spell
I would hit you over the head with it,
so that you would get well.

Qt clown

Okay you're probably wondering what this clown thing is all about. Heather decided one day out of the blue she wanted to be a clown. She went on e-Bay and bought a clown costume and clown shoes. The stuff all arrived at the house and she was in her glory. Heather was surfing the net one Friday afternoon and discovered there was a clown college in Edmonton that weekend so she registered and we left right away as the boys were with their dad's for a visit so we had no worries. Heather enjoyed the course and I had fun with Tim and my mom. Heather attended another course in Calgary a couple of months later. Her clown name is QT Clown and she enjoys doing it.

On the weekend I got released from hospital August 1st Heather had an engagement for the annual Bruno cherry festival. She worked both the Saturday and Sunday. Heather had also arranged for me to do a reading from Bipolar Shoes and I didn't know if I could do it. She came with me for moral support. Fittingly it was in the chapel that the event took place. There were three other authors present and we each had fifteen minutes my presentation would be second. There were roughly fifteen people in attendance.

I was introduced to the audience then I welcomed everyone and conveyed my appreciation for the chance to tell my story. I also made it clear that this was the first time I had talked about Bipolar Shoes and bipolar disorder in a public venue. I read the story "Anything's Possible" that is at the front of this book and I got Heather to read the introduction. I was shaking pretty good as I was reading, and they had only a music stand so there was nothing to lean on. I was approached by everyone after the event wishing me well with Bipolar Shoes and they gave me words of encouragement in my attempt to bring awareness to bipolar disorder. A few people said it was courageous the way I spoke about my life. Others said the personal touch from the perspective of an ordinary person sharing their story was moving.

Heather no doubt is my number one fan she has given me the support and strength to carry on with life. We don't talk very much about happened to me, we just move forward to challenge the next day. I remember the first time I seen Heather as a clown in public it was for the walk of hope for Cancer. Heather and the boys along with Maggie participated in this event.

I walked from home at 3:30 in the morning to the parking lot of the Uniplex I could hear music as I walked and the sounds of people talking on microphones. When I arrived they had a track made around the parking lot with candles. I was surprised to see so many people walking and all of them in Great Spirit at that time of the night. I found our van and the makeshift campsite Heather and the boys had created. Maggie was sitting in a lawn chair and I joined her. She was telling me about the event and how it worked. I saw Heather having fun as she walked and carried on like a clown with a big group of people.

When I talked to Heather she was full of energy and had a glow to her that I noticed I hadn't seen in a very long time. She was thrilled that people accepted her as a clown and that everyone was enjoying her antics. Heather and Maggie are both Cancer survivors so this was a very emotional event for them. I will never forget the look of magic in Heather that night nor the sheer excitement she expressed to me. It was a special moment for me to see my wife doing what she wanted by being a clown. Heather is a fantastic clown who makes people happy by being herself. She made me realize something was wrong and she took care of the situation. QT clown is a terrific extension of a beautiful person who is innocent by nature. I have been blessed by God to have our paths cross in this life as it was by chance that we met in the first place.

In finishing this book I feel it is only fitting that it ends the same way as it started. The title "Anything's" Possible was made a reality by the determination of both Heather and me. She has never given up or lost faith in me even when the chips were down and everything was looking bleak. While I was in the hospital they would put a quote on the board every day, I would like to share a couple that I thought were good.

If you can imagine it, you can achieve it.
If you can dream it, you can become it.
> **William Arthur Ward**

The future depends on what we do in the present.
> **Gandhi**

Anything is possible when you truly believe in yourself,
> **Dave O'Riordan**

I need to thank a few people for making this project possible.

First, I would like to thank my mother, Pat, for always believing in me; she knows me better than most. Without her support this book would not have been possible. Thanks mom for making Bipolar Shoes available to people who may benefit from it and for knowing how important this project was to me.

My best friends, Tim Johnson and his wife Tammy, we always share a laugh. Tim has always been a true friend. I love you guys, you too Kelly. Yes you too Larry love you buddy.

My daughters, Angela, and Deirdre, Have started families of their own and now enjoy the responsibilities of being parents. They both have always made me proud and always inspire me. They made the trip to Humboldt and Saskatoon to visit me while I was in hospital. They brought three of the children with them. I know that was no easy feat and I know they did it just for me.

My four stepsons, Cody, Robert, Travis, and Tyler, for trying my patience and letting me remember what it's like to be a kid. I am lucky to be associated with four fine young men.

I saved the best for last, and that is my wife, Heather. She inspired me to do something with my time and supported me all the way through this project. Heather has learned about bipolar disorder and tolerates me for who I am. I know I am fortunate to have her in my life; she definitely keeps me grounded. "You and Me" always, I love you.

I know I'm not a big star or athlete, but I do want to thank God, Jesus, and the Holy Spirit. They guided me through this project. There were many times my fingers just punched the letters and amazing stuff came off. I wrote a song for my wedding that I called "My Lighthouse," and God is definitely my beacon of hope.

I would like to let my daughter Cassandra, know that I feel her pain and I hope that we can be close again someday. Cassie I think about you every day and hope you are doing well. The letters you sent me by e-mail made me realize what you are going through. I want you to know that I love you and I'll always have you in my heart. My door will always be open to you and I understand why you have shut yours. Along this journey of life I forgot that you too maybe dealing with some issues. I am always here when you are ready. I pray that you are doing well.

Finally, Thank you for purchasing or reading Bipolar Shoes, you have made a small contribution to mental health. It may not be monetary and that's okay, however you are a bit more aware so you may be able to assist someone and help them. Every little bit helps "thank you ever so much." Dave

Bipolar Disorder

Introduction:

This booklet discusses bipolar disorder in adults. For information on bipolar disorder in children and adolescents, see the NIMH booklet, "Bipolar Disorder in Children and Teens: A Parent's Guide."

What is bipolar disorder?

Bipolar disorder, also known as manic-depressive illness, is a brain disorder that causes unusual shifts in mood, energy, activity levels, and the ability to carry out day-to-day tasks. Symptoms of bipolar disorder are severe. They are different from the normal ups and downs that everyone goes through from time to time. Bipolar disorder symptoms can result in damaged relationships, poor job or school performance, and even suicide. But bipolar disorder can be treated, and people with this illness can lead full and productive lives.

Bipolar disorder often develops in a person's late teens or early adult years. At least half of all cases start before age 25.[1] Some people have their first symptoms during childhood, while others may develop symptoms late in life.

Bipolar disorder is not easy to spot when it starts. The symptoms may seem like separate problems, not recognized as parts of a larger problem. Some people suffer for years before they are properly diagnosed and treated. Like diabetes or heart disease, bipolar disorder is a long-term illness that must be carefully managed throughout a person's life.

146

What are the symptoms of bipolar disorder?

People with bipolar disorder experience unusually intense emotional states that occur in distinct periods called "mood episodes." An overly joyful or overexcited state is called a manic episode, and an extremely sad or hopeless state is called a depressive episode. Sometimes, a mood episode includes symptoms of both mania and depression. This is called a mixed state. People with bipolar disorder also may be explosive and irritable during a mood episode.

Extreme changes in energy, activity, sleep, and behavior go along with these changes in mood. It is possible for someone with bipolar disorder to experience a long-lasting period of unstable moods rather than discrete episodes of depression or mania.

A person may be having an episode of bipolar disorder if he or she has a number of manic or depressive symptoms for most of the day, nearly every day, for at least one or two weeks. Sometimes symptoms are so severe that the person cannot function normally at work, school, or home.

Symptoms of bipolar disorder are described below.

Symptoms of mania or a manic episode include:	**Symptoms of depression or a depressive episode include:**

Mood Changes

Mood Changes

- A long period of feeling "high," or an overly happy or outgoing mood
- Extremely irritable mood, agitation, feeling "jumpy" or "wired."

- A long period of feeling worried or empty
- Loss of interest in activities once enjoyed, including sex.

Behavioral Changes

Behavioral Changes

- Talking very fast, jumping from one idea to another, having racing thoughts
- Being easily distracted
- Increasing goal-directed activities, such as taking on new projects
- Being restless
- Sleeping little
- Having an unrealistic belief in one's abilities
- Behaving impulsively and taking part in a lot of pleasurable, high-risk behaviors, such as spending sprees, impulsive sex, and impulsive business investments.

- Feeling tired or "slowed down"
- Having problems concentrating, remembering, and making decisions
- Being restless or irritable
- Changing eating, sleeping, or other habits
- Thinking of death or suicide, or attempting suicide.

In addition to mania and depression, bipolar disorder can cause a range of moods, as shown on the scale.

One side of the scale includes severe depression, moderate depression, and mild low mood. Moderate depression may cause less extreme symptoms, and mild low mood is called dysthymia when it is chronic or long-term. In the middle of the scale is normal or balanced mood.

At the other end of the scale are hypomania and severe mania. Some people with bipolar disorder experience hypomania. During hypomanic episodes, a person may have increased energy and activity levels that are not as severe as typical mania, or he or she may have episodes that last less than a week and do not require emergency care. A person having a hypomanic episode may feel very good, be highly productive, and function well. This person may not feel that anything is wrong even as family and friends recognize the mood swings as possible bipolar disorder. Without proper treatment, however, people with hypomania may develop severe mania or depression.

During a mixed state, symptoms often include agitation, trouble sleeping, major changes in appetite, and suicidal thinking. People in a mixed state may feel very sad or hopeless while feeling extremely energized.

Sometimes, a person with severe episodes of mania or depression has psychotic symptoms too, such as hallucinations or delusions. The psychotic symptoms tend to reflect the person's extreme mood. For example, psychotic symptoms for a person having a manic episode may include believing he or she is famous, has a lot of money, or has special powers. In the same way, a person having a depressive episode may believe he or she is ruined and penniless, or has committed a crime. As a result, people with bipolar disorder who have psychotic symptoms are sometimes wrongly diagnosed as having schizophrenia, another severe mental illness that is linked with hallucinations and delusions.

People with bipolar disorder may also have behavioral problems. They may abuse alcohol or substances, have relationship problems, or perform poorly in school or at work. At first, it's not easy to recognize these problems as signs of a major mental illness.

How does bipolar disorder affect someone over time?

Bipolar disorder usually lasts a lifetime. Episodes of mania and depression typically come back over time. Between episodes, many people with bipolar disorder are free of symptoms, but some people may have lingering symptoms.

Doctors usually diagnose mental disorders using guidelines from the *Diagnostic and Statistical Manual of Mental Disorders*, or DSM. According to the DSM, there are four basic types of bipolar disorder:

1. **Bipolar I Disorder** is mainly defined by manic or mixed episodes that last at least seven days, or by manic symptoms that are so severe that the person needs immediate hospital care. Usually, the person also has depressive episodes, typically lasting at least two weeks. The symptoms of mania or depression must be a major change from the person's normal behavior.

2. **Bipolar II Disorder** is defined by a pattern of depressive episodes shifting back and forth with hypomanic episodes, but no full-blown manic or mixed episodes.

3. **Bipolar Disorder Not Otherwise Specified (BP-NOS)** is diagnosed when a person has symptoms of the illness that do not meet diagnostic criteria for either bipolar I or II. The symptoms may not last long enough, or the person may have too few symptoms, to be diagnosed with bipolar I or II. However, the symptoms are clearly out of the person's normal range of behavior.

4. **Cyclothymic Disorder, or Cyclothymia**, is a mild form of bipolar disorder. People who have cyclothymia have episodes of hypomania that shift back and forth with mild depression for at least two years. However, the symptoms do not meet the diagnostic requirements for any other type of bipolar disorder.

Some people may be diagnosed with **rapid-cycling bipolar disorder**. This is when a person has four or more episodes of major depression, mania, hypomania, or mixed symptoms within a year.[2] Some people experience more than one episode in a week, or even within one day. Rapid cycling seems to be more common in people who have severe bipolar disorder and may be more common in people who have their first episode at a younger age. One study found that people with rapid cycling had their first episode about four years earlier, during mid to late teen years, than people without rapid cycling bipolar disorder.[3] Rapid cycling affects more women than men.[4]

Bipolar disorder tends to worsen if it is not treated. Over time, a person may suffer more frequent and more severe episodes than when the illness first appeared.[5] Also, delays in getting the correct diagnosis and treatment make a person more likely to experience personal, social, and work-related problems.[6]

Proper diagnosis and treatment helps people with bipolar disorder lead healthy and productive lives. In most cases, treatment can help reduce the frequency and severity of episodes.

What illnesses often co-exist with bipolar disorder?

Substance abuse is very common among people with bipolar disorder, but the reasons for this link are unclear.[7] Some people with bipolar disorder may try to treat their symptoms with alcohol or drugs. However, substance abuse may trigger or prolong bipolar symptoms, and the behavioral control problems associated with mania can result in a person drinking too much.

Anxiety disorders, such as post-traumatic stress disorder (PTSD) and social phobia, also co-occur often among people with bipolar disorder.[8-10] Bipolar disorder also co-occurs with attention deficit hyperactivity disorder (ADHD), which has some symptoms that overlap with bipolar disorder, such as restlessness and being easily distracted.

People with bipolar disorder are also at higher risk for thyroid disease, migraine headaches, heart disease, diabetes, obesity, and other physical illnesses.[10, 11] These illnesses may cause symptoms of mania or depression. They may also result from treatment for bipolar disorder.

Other illnesses can make it hard to diagnose and treat bipolar disorder. People with bipolar disorder should monitor their physical and mental health. If a symptom does not get better with treatment, they should tell their doctor.

What are the risk factors for bipolar disorder?

Scientists are learning about the possible causes of bipolar disorder. Most scientists agree that there is no single cause. Rather, many factors likely act together to produce the illness or increase risk.

Genetics

Bipolar disorder tends to run in families, so researchers are looking for genes that may increase a person's chance of developing the illness. Genes are the "building blocks" of heredity. They help control how the body and brain work and grow. Genes are contained inside a person's cells that are passed down from parents to children.

Children with a parent or sibling who has bipolar disorder are four to six times more likely to develop the illness, compared with children who do not have a family history of bipolar disorder.[12] However, most children with a family history of bipolar disorder will not develop the illness.

Genetic research on bipolar disorder is being helped by advances in technology. This type of research is now much quicker and more far-reaching than in the past. One example is the launch of the Bipolar Disorder Phenome Database, funded in part by NIMH. Using the database, scientists will be able to link visible signs of the disorder with the genes that may influence them. So far, researchers using this database found that most people with bipolar disorder had:[13]

- Missed work because of their illness
- Other illnesses at the same time, especially alcohol and/or substance abuse and panic disorders
- Been treated or hospitalized for bipolar disorder.

The researchers also identified certain traits that appeared to run in families, including:

- History of psychiatric hospitalization
- Co-occurring obsessive-compulsive disorder (OCD)
- Age at first manic episode
- Number and frequency of manic episodes.

Scientists continue to study these traits, which may help them find the genes that cause bipolar disorder some day.

But genes are not the only risk factor for bipolar disorder. Studies of identical twins have shown that the twin of a person with bipolar illness does not always develop the disorder. This is important because identical twins share all of the same genes. The study results suggest factors besides genes are also at work. Rather, it is likely that many different genes and a person's environment are involved. However, scientists do not yet fully understand how these factors interact to cause bipolar disorder.

Brain structure and functioning

Brain-imaging studies are helping scientists learn what happens in the brain of a person with bipolar disorder.[14, 15] Newer brain-imaging tools, such as functional magnetic resonance imaging (fMRI) and positron emission tomography (PET), allow researchers to take pictures of the living brain at work. These tools help scientists study the brain's structure and activity.

Some imaging studies show how the brains of people with bipolar disorder may differ from the brains of healthy people or people with other mental disorders. For example, one study using MRI found that the pattern of brain development in children with bipolar disorder was similar to that in children with "multi-dimensional impairment," a disorder that causes symptoms that overlap somewhat with bipolar disorder and schizophrenia.[16] This suggests that the common pattern of brain development may be linked to general risk for unstable moods.

Learning more about these differences, along with information gained from genetic studies, helps scientists better understand bipolar disorder. Someday scientists may be able to predict which types of treatment will work most effectively. They may even find ways to prevent bipolar disorder.

How is bipolar disorder diagnosed?

The first step in getting a proper diagnosis is to talk to a doctor, who may conduct a physical examination, an interview, and lab tests. Bipolar disorder cannot currently be identified through a blood test or a brain scan, but these tests can help rule out other contributing factors, such as a stroke or brain tumor. If the problems are not caused by other illnesses, the doctor may conduct a mental health evaluation. The doctor may also provide a referral to a trained mental health professional, such as a psychiatrist, who is experienced in diagnosing and treating bipolar disorder.

The doctor or mental health professional should conduct a complete diagnostic evaluation. He or she should discuss any family history of bipolar disorder or other mental illnesses and get a complete history of symptoms. The doctor or mental health professionals should also talk to the person's close relatives or spouse and note how they describe the person's symptoms and family medical history.

People with bipolar disorder are more likely to seek help when they are depressed than when experiencing mania or hypomania.[17] Therefore, a careful medical history is needed to assure that bipolar disorder is not mistakenly diagnosed as major depressive disorder, which is also called unipolar depression. Unlike people with bipolar disorder, people who have unipolar depression do not experience mania. Whenever possible, previous records and input from family and friends should also be included in the medical history.

How is bipolar disorder treated?

To date, there is no cure for bipolar disorder. But proper treatment helps most people with bipolar disorder gain better control of their mood swings and related symptoms.[18-20] This is also true for people with the most severe forms of the illness.

Because bipolar disorder is a lifelong and recurrent illness, people with the disorder need long-term treatment to maintain control of bipolar symptoms. An effective maintenance treatment plan includes medication and psychotherapy for preventing relapse and reducing symptom severity.[21]

Medications

Bipolar disorder can be diagnosed and medications prescribed by people with an M.D. (doctor of medicine). Usually, bipolar medications are prescribed by a psychiatrist. In some states, clinical psychologists, psychiatric nurse practitioners, and advanced psychiatric nurse specialists can also prescribe medications. Check with your state's licensing agency to find out more.

Not everyone responds to medications in the same way. Several different medications may need to be tried before the best course of treatment is found.

Keeping a chart of daily mood symptoms, treatments, sleep patterns, and life events can help the doctor track and treat the illness most effectively. Sometimes this is called a daily life chart. If a person's symptoms change or if side effects become serious, the doctor may switch or add medications.

Some of the types of medications generally used to treat bipolar disorder are listed on the next page. Information on medications can change. For the most up to date information on use and side effects contact the U.S. Food and Drug Administration (FDA).

1. **Mood stabilizing medications** are usually the first choice to treat bipolar disorder. In general, people with bipolar disorder continue treatment with mood stabilizers for years. Except for lithium, many of these medications are anticonvulsants. Anticonvulsant medications are usually used to treat seizures, but they also help control moods. These medications are commonly used as mood stabilizers in bipolar disorder:

   - Lithium (sometimes known as Eskalith or Lithobid) was the first mood-stabilizing medication approved by the U.S. Food and Drug Administration (FDA) in the 1970s for treatment of mania. It is often very effective in controlling symptoms of mania and preventing the recurrence of manic and depressive episodes.
   - Valproic acid or divalproex sodium (Depakote), approved by the FDA in 1995 for treating mania, is a popular alternative to lithium for bipolar disorder. It is generally as effective as lithium

for treating bipolar disorder.[23, 24] Also see the section in this booklet, "Should young women take valproic acid?"

- More recently, the anticonvulsant lamotrigine (Lamictal) received FDA approval for maintenance treatment of bipolar disorder.
- Other anticonvulsant medications, including gabapentin (Neurontin), topiramate (Topamax), and oxcarbazepine (Trileptal) are sometimes prescribed. No large studies have shown that these medications are more effective than mood stabilizers.

Valproic acid, lamotrigine, and other anticonvulsant medications have an FDA warning. The warning states that their use may increase the risk of suicidal thoughts and behaviors. People taking anticonvulsant medications for bipolar or other illnesses should be closely monitored for new or worsening symptoms of depression, suicidal thoughts or behavior, or any unusual changes in mood or behavior. People taking these medications should not make any changes without talking to their health care professional.

Lithium and Thyroid Function

People with bipolar disorder often have thyroid gland problems. Lithium treatment may also cause low thyroid levels in some people.[22] Low thyroid function, called hypothyroidism, has been associated with rapid cycling in some people with bipolar disorder, especially women.

Because too much or too little thyroid hormone can lead to mood and energy changes, it is important to have a doctor check thyroid levels carefully. A person with bipolar disorder may need to take thyroid medication, in addition to medications for bipolar disorder, to keep thyroid levels balanced.

Should young women take valproic acid?

Valproic acid may increase levels of testosterone (a male hormone) in teenage girls and lead to polycystic ovary syndrome (PCOS) in women who begin taking the medication before age 20.[25, 26] PCOS causes a woman's eggs to develop into cysts, or fluid filled sacs that collect in the ovaries instead of being released by monthly periods. This condition can cause obesity, excess body hair, disruptions in the menstrual cycle, and other serious symptoms. Most of these symptoms will improve after stopping treatment with valproic acid.[27] Young girls and women taking valproic acid should be monitored carefully by a doctor.

2. **Atypical antipsychotic medications** are sometimes used to treat symptoms of bipolar disorder. Often, these medications are taken with other medications. Atypical antipsychotic medications are called "atypical" to set them apart from earlier medications, which are called "conventional" or "first-generation" antipsychotics.

- Olanzapine (Zyprexa), when given with an antidepressant medication, may help relieve symptoms of severe mania or psychosis.[28] Olanzapine is also available in an injectable form, which quickly treats agitation associated with a manic or mixed episode. Olanzapine can be used for maintenance treatment of bipolar disorder as well, even when a person does not have psychotic symptoms. However, some studies show that people taking olanzapine may gain weight and have other side effects that can increase their risk for diabetes and heart disease. These side effects are more likely in people taking olanzapine when compared with people prescribed other atypical antipsychotics.
- Aripiprazole (Abilify), like olanzapine, is approved for treatment of a manic or mixed episode. Aripiprazole is also used for maintenance treatment after a severe or sudden episode. As with olanzapine, aripiprazole also can be injected for urgent

treatment of symptoms of manic or mixed episodes of bipolar disorder.

- Quetiapine (Seroquel) relieves the symptoms of severe and sudden manic episodes. In that way, quetiapine is like almost all antipsychotics. In 2006, it became the first atypical antipsychotic to also receive FDA approval for the treatment of bipolar depressive episodes.

- Risperidone (Risperdal) and ziprasidone (Geodon) are other atypical antipsychotics that may also be prescribed for controlling manic or mixed episodes.

3. **Antidepressant medications** are sometimes used to treat symptoms of depression in bipolar disorder. People with bipolar disorder who take antidepressants often take a mood stabilizer too. Doctors usually require this because taking only an antidepressant can increase a person's risk of switching to mania or hypomania, or of developing rapid cycling symptoms.[29] To prevent this switch, doctors who prescribe antidepressants for treating bipolar disorder also usually require the person to take a mood-stabilizing medication at the same time.

Recently, a large-scale, NIMH-funded study showed that for many people, adding an antidepressant to a mood stabilizer is no more effective in treating the depression than using only a mood stabilizer.[30]

- Fluoxetine (Prozac), paroxetine (Paxil), sertraline (Zoloft), and bupropion (Wellbutrin) are examples of antidepressants that may be prescribed to treat symptoms of bipolar depression.

Some medications are better at treating one type of bipolar symptoms than another. For example, lamotrigine (Lamictal) seems to be helpful in controlling depressive symptoms of bipolar disorder.

What are the side effects of these medications?

Before starting a new medication, people with bipolar disorder should talk to their doctor about the possible risks and benefits.

The psychiatrist prescribing the medication or pharmacist can also answer questions about side effects. Over the last decade, treatments have improved, and some medications now have fewer or more tolerable side effects than earlier treatments. However, everyone responds differently to medications. In some cases, side effects may not appear until a person has taken a medication for some time.

If the person with bipolar disorder develops any severe side effects from a medication, he or she should talk to the doctor who prescribed it as soon as possible. The doctor may change the dose or prescribe a different medication. People being treated for bipolar disorder should not stop taking a medication without talking to a doctor first. Suddenly stopping a medication may lead to "rebound," or worsening of bipolar disorder symptoms. Other uncomfortable or potentially dangerous withdrawal effects are also possible.

FDA Warning on Antidepressants

Antidepressants are safe and popular, but some studies have suggested that they may have unintentional effects on some people, especially in adolescents and young adults. The FDA warning says that patients of all ages taking antidepressants should be watched closely, especially during the first few weeks of treatment. Possible side effects to look for are depression that gets worse, suicidal thinking or behavior, or any unusual changes in behavior such as trouble sleeping, agitation, or withdrawal from normal social situations. Families and caregivers should report any changes to the doctor. For the latest information visit the FDA website.

The following sections describe some common side effects of the different types of medications used to treat bipolar disorder.

1. Mood Stabilizers

In some cases, lithium can cause side effects such as:

- Restlessness
- Dry mouth
- Bloating or indigestion
- Acne
- Unusual discomfort to cold temperatures
- Joint or muscle pain
- Brittle nails or hair.[31]

Lithium also causes side effects not listed here. If extremely bothersome or unusual side effects occur, tell your doctor as soon as possible.

If a person with bipolar disorder is being treated with lithium, it is important to make regular visits to the treating doctor. The doctor needs to check the levels of lithium in the person's blood, as well as kidney and thyroid function.

These medications may also be linked with rare but serious side effects. Talk with the treating doctor or a pharmacist to make sure you understand signs of serious side effects for the medications you're taking.

Common side effects of other mood stabilizing medications include:

- Drowsiness
- Dizziness
- Headache
- Diarrhea
- Constipation
- Heartburn
- Mood swings
- Stuffed or runny nose, or other cold-like symptoms.[32-37]

2. Atypical Antipsychotics

Some people have side effects when they start taking atypical antipsychotics. Most side effects go away after a few days and often can be managed successfully. People who are taking antipsychotics should not drive until they adjust to their new medication. Side effects of many antipsychotics include:

- Drowsiness
- Dizziness when changing positions
- Blurred vision
- Rapid heartbeat
- Sensitivity to the sun
- Skin rashes
- Menstrual problems for women.

Atypical antipsychotic medications can cause major weight gain and changes in a person's metabolism. This may increase a person's risk of getting diabetes and high cholesterol.[38] A person's weight, glucose levels, and lipid levels should be monitored regularly by a doctor while taking these medications.

In rare cases, long-term use of atypical antipsychotic drugs may lead to a condition called tardive dyskinesia (TD). The condition causes muscle movements that commonly occur around the mouth. A person with TD cannot control these moments. TD can range from mild to severe, and it cannot always be cured. Some people with TD recover partially or fully after they stop taking the drug.

3. Antidepressants

The antidepressants most commonly prescribed for treating symptoms of bipolar disorder can also cause mild side effects that usually do not last long. These can include:

- Headache, which usually goes away within a few days.

- Nausea (feeling sick to your stomach), which usually goes away within a few days.
- Sleep problems, such as sleeplessness or drowsiness. This may happen during the first few weeks but then go away. To help lessen these effects, sometimes the medication dose can be reduced, or the time of day it is taken can be changed.
- Agitation (feeling jittery).
- Sexual problems, which can affect both men and women. These include reduced sex drive and problems having and enjoying sex.

Some antidepressants are more likely to cause certain side effects than other types. Your doctor or pharmacist can answer questions about these medications. Any unusual reactions or side effects should be reported to a doctor immediately.

For the most up-to-date information on medications for treating bipolar disorder and their side effects, please see the online NIMH Medications booklet.

Should women who are pregnant or may become pregnant take medication for bipolar disorder?

Women with bipolar disorder who are pregnant or may become pregnant face special challenges. The mood stabilizing medications in use today can harm a developing fetus or nursing infant.[39] But stopping medications, either suddenly or gradually, greatly increases the risk that bipolar symptoms will recur during pregnancy.[40]

Scientists are not sure yet, but lithium is likely the preferred mood-stabilizing medication for pregnant women with bipolar disorder.[40, 41] However, lithium can lead to heart problems in the fetus. Women need to know that most bipolar medications are passed on through breast milk.[41] Pregnant women and nursing mothers should talk to their doctors about the benefits and risks of all available treatments.

Psychotherapy

In addition to medication, psychotherapy, or "talk" therapy, can be an effective treatment for bipolar disorder. It can provide support, education, and guidance to people with bipolar disorder and their families. Some psychotherapy treatments used to treat bipolar disorder include:

1. **Cognitive behavioral therapy (CBT)** helps people with bipolar disorder learn to change harmful or negative thought patterns and behaviors.
2. **Family-focused therapy** includes family members. It helps enhance family coping strategies, such as recognizing new episodes early and helping their loved one. This therapy also improves communication and problem-solving.
3. **Interpersonal and social rhythm therapy** helps people with bipolar disorder improve their relationships with others and manage their daily routines. Regular daily routines and sleep schedules may help protect against manic episodes.
4. **Psychoeducation** teaches people with bipolar disorder about the illness and its treatment. This treatment helps people recognize signs of relapse so they can seek treatment early, before a full-blown episode occurs. Usually done in a group, psychoeducation may also be helpful for family members and caregivers.

A licensed psychologist, social worker, or counselor typically provides these therapies. This mental health professional often works with the psychiatrist to track progress. The number, frequency, and type of sessions should be based on the treatment needs of each person. As with medication, following the doctor's instructions for any psychotherapy will provide the greatest benefit.

For more information, see the <u>Substance Abuse and Mental Health Services Administration</u> web page on choosing a mental health therapist.

Recently, NIMH funded a clinical trial called the <u>Systematic Treatment Enhancement Program for Bipolar Disorder (STEP-BD)</u>. This was the largest treatment study ever conducted for bipolar disorder. In a study on psychotherapies, STEP-BD researchers compared people in two groups. The first group was treated with collaborative care (three sessions of psychoeducation over six weeks). The second group was treated with medication and intensive psychotherapy (30 sessions over nine months of CBT, interpersonal and social rhythm therapy, or family-focused therapy). Researchers found that the second group had fewer relapses, lower hospitalization rates, and were better able to stick with their treatment plans.[42] They were also more likely to get well faster and stay well longer.

NIMH is supporting more research on which combinations of psychotherapy and medication work best. The goal is to help people with bipolar disorder live symptom-free for longer periods and to recover from episodes more quickly. Researchers also hope to determine whether psychotherapy helps delay the start of bipolar disorder in children at high risk for the illness.

Visit the NIMH Web site for more information on <u>psychotherapy</u>.

Other treatments

1. **Electroconvulsive Therapy (ECT)**—For cases in which medication and/or psychotherapy does not work, electroconvulsive therapy (ECT) may be useful. ECT, formerly known as "shock therapy," once had a bad reputation. But in recent years, it has greatly improved and can provide relief for people with severe bipolar disorder who have not been able to feel better with other treatments.

    Before ECT is administered, a patient takes a muscle relaxant and is put under brief anesthesia. He or she does not consciously feel the electrical impulse administered in ECT. On average,

ECT treatments last from 30–90 seconds. People who have ECT usually recover after 5–15 minutes and are able to go home the same day.[43]

Sometimes ECT is used for bipolar symptoms when other medical conditions, including pregnancy, make the use of medications too risky. ECT is a highly effective treatment for severely depressive, manic, or mixed episodes, but is generally not a first-line treatment.

ECT may cause some short-term side effects, including confusion, disorientation, and memory loss. But these side effects typically clear soon after treatment. People with bipolar disorder should discuss possible benefits and risks of ECT with an experienced doctor.[44]

2. **Sleep Medications**—People with bipolar disorder who have trouble sleeping usually sleep better after getting treatment for bipolar disorder. However, if sleeplessness does not improve, the doctor may suggest a change in medications. If the problems still continue, the doctor may prescribe sedatives or other sleep medications.

People with bipolar disorder should tell their doctor about all prescription drugs, over-the-counter medications, or supplements they are taking. Certain medications and supplements taken together may cause unwanted or dangerous effects.

Herbal Supplements

In general, there is not much research about herbal or natural supplements. Little is known about their effects on bipolar disorder. An herb called St. John's wort (*Hypericum perforatum*), often marketed as a natural antidepressant, may cause a switch to mania in some people with bipolar disorder.[45] St. John's wort can also make other medications less effective, including some antidepressant and anticonvulsant medications.[46] Scientists are also researching omega-3 fatty acids (most commonly found in fish oil) to measure their usefulness for long-term treatment of bipolar disorder.[47] Study results have been mixed.[48] It is important to talk with a doctor before taking any herbal or natural supplements because of the serious risk of interactions with other medications.

What can people with bipolar disorder expect from treatment?

Bipolar disorder has no cure, but can be effectively treated over the long-term. It is best controlled when treatment is continuous, rather than on and off. In the STEP-BD study, a little more than half of the people treated for bipolar disorder recovered over one year's time. For this study, recovery meant having two or fewer symptoms of the disorder for at least eight weeks.

However, even with proper treatment, mood changes can occur. In the STEP-BD study, almost half of those who recovered still had lingering symptoms. These people experienced a relapse or recurrence that was usually a return to a depressive state.[49] If a person had a mental illness in addition to bipolar disorder, he or she was more likely to experience a relapse.[49] Scientists are unsure, however, how these other illnesses or lingering symptoms increase the chance of relapse. For some people, combining psychotherapy with medication may help to prevent or delay relapse.[42]

Treatment may be more effective when people work closely with a doctor and talk openly about their concerns and choices. Keeping track of mood changes and symptoms with a daily life chart can help a doctor assess a person's response to treatments. Sometimes the doctor needs to change a treatment plan to make sure symptoms are controlled most effectively. A psychiatrist should guide any changes in type or dose of medication.

How can I help a friend or relative who has bipolar disorder?

If you know someone who has bipolar disorder, it affects you too. The first and most important thing you can do is help him or her get the right diagnosis and treatment. You may need to make the appointment and go with him or her to see the doctor. Encourage your loved one to stay in treatment.

To help a friend or relative, you can:

- Offer emotional support, understanding, patience, and encouragement
- Learn about bipolar disorder so you can understand what your friend or relative is experiencing
- Talk to your friend or relative and listen carefully
- Listen to feelings your friend or relative expresses-be understanding about situations that may trigger bipolar symptoms
- Invite your friend or relative out for positive distractions, such as walks, outings, and other activities
- Remind your friend or relative that, with time and treatment, he or she can get better.

Never ignore comments about your friend or relative harming himself or herself. Always report such comments to his or her therapist or doctor.

Support for caregivers

Like other serious illnesses, bipolar disorder can be difficult for spouses, family members, friends, and other caregivers. Relatives and friends often have to cope with the person's serious behavioral problems, such as wild spending sprees during mania, extreme withdrawal during depression, poor work or school performance. These behaviors can have lasting consequences.

Caregivers usually take care of the medical needs of their loved ones. The caregivers have to deal with how this affects their own health. The stress that caregivers are under may lead to missed work or lost free time, strained relationships with people who may not understand the situation, and physical and mental exhaustion.

Stress from caregiving can make it hard to cope with a loved one's bipolar symptoms. One study shows that if a caregiver is under a lot of stress, his or her loved one has more trouble following the treatment plan, which increases the chance for a major bipolar episode.[50] It is important that people caring for those with bipolar disorder also take care of themselves.

How can I help myself if I have bipolar disorder?

It may be very hard to take that first step to help yourself. It may take time, but you can get better with treatment.

To help yourself:

- Talk to your doctor about treatment options and progress
- Keep a regular routine, such as eating meals at the same time every day and going to sleep at the same time every night
- Try to get enough sleep
- Stay on your medication
- Learn about warning signs signaling a shift into depression or mania
- Expect your symptoms to improve gradually, not immediately.

Where can I go for help?

If you are unsure where to go for help, ask your family doctor. Others who can help are listed below.

- Mental health specialists, such as psychiatrists, psychologists, social workers, or mental health counselors

169

- Health maintenance organizations
- Community mental health centers
- Hospital psychiatry departments and outpatient clinics
- Mental health programs at universities or medical schools
- State hospital outpatient clinics
- Family services, social agencies, or clergy
- Peer support groups
- Private clinics and facilities
- Employee assistance programs
- Local medical and/or psychiatric societies.

You can also check the phone book under "mental health," "health," "social services," "hotlines," or "physicians" for phone numbers and addresses. An emergency room doctor can also provide temporary help and can tell you where and how to get further help.

What if I or someone I know is in crisis?

If you are thinking about harming yourself, or know someone who is, tell someone who can help immediately.

- Call your doctor.
- Call 911 or go to a hospital emergency room to get immediate help or ask a friend or family member to help you do these things.
- Call the toll-free, 24-hour hotline of the National Suicide Prevention Lifeline at 1-800-273-TALK (1-800-273-8255); TTY: 1-800-799-4TTY (4889) to talk to a trained counselor.

Make sure you or the suicidal person is not left alone.

Citations

1. Kessler RC, Berglund P, Demler O, Jin R, Merikangas KR, Walters EE. Lifetime prevalence and age-of-onset distributions of DSM-IV disorders in the National Comorbidity Survey Replication. *Arch Gen Psychiatry.* 2005 Jun;62(6):593-602.

2. Akiskal HS. "Mood Disorders: Clinical Features." in Sadock BJ, Sadock VA (ed). (2005). *Kaplan & Sadock's Comprehensive Textbook of Psychiatry.* Lippincott Williams & Wilkins:Philadelphia.

3. Schneck CD, Miklowitz DJ, Miyahara S, Araga M, Wisniewski S, Gyulai L, Allen MH, Thase ME, Sachs GS. The prospective course of rapid-cycling bipolar disorder: findings from the STEP-BD. *Am J Psychiatry.* 2008 Mar;165(3):370-7; quiz 410.

4. Schneck CD, Miklowitz DJ, Calabrese JR, Allen MH, Thomas MR, Wisniewski SR, Miyahara S, Shelton MD, Ketter TA, Goldberg JF, Bowden CL, Sachs GS. Phenomenology of rapid-cycling bipolar disorder: data from the first 500 participants in the Systematic Treatment Enhancement Program. *Am J Psychiatry.* 2004 Oct;161(10):1902-1908.

5. Goodwin FK, Jamison KR. (2007) *Manic-Depressive Illness: Bipolar Disorders and Recurrent Depression, Second Edition.* Oxford University Press:New York.

6. *Constituency Survey: Living With Bipolar Disorder: How Far Have We Really Come?* National Depressive and Manic-Depressive Association. 2001.

7. Bizzarri JV, Sbrana A, Rucci P, Ravani L, Massei GJ, Gonnelli C, Spagnolli S, Doria MR, Raimondi F, Endicott J, Dell'Osso L, Cassano GB. The spectrum of substance abuse in bipolar disorder: reasons for use, sensation seeking and substance sensitivity. *Bipolar Disord.* 2007 May;9(3):213-220.

8. Mueser KT, Goodman LB, Trumbetta SL, Rosenberg SD, Osher C, Vidaver R, Auciello P, Foy DW. Trauma and posttraumatic stress disorder in severe mental illness. *J Consult Clin Psychol.* 1998 Jun;66(3):493-499.

9. Strakowski SM, Sax KW, McElroy SL, Keck PE, Jr., Hawkins JM, West SA. Course of psychiatric and substance abuse syndromes co-occurring with bipolar disorder after a first psychiatric hospitalization. *J Consult Clin Psychol.* 1998 Sep;59(9):465-471.

10. Krishnan KR. Psychiatric and medical comorbidities of bipolar disorder. *Psychosom Med.* 2005 Jan-Feb;67(1):1-8.

11. Kupfer DJ. The increasing medical burden in bipolar disorder. *JAMA.* 2005 May 25;293(20):2528-2530.

12. Nurnberger JI, Jr., Foroud T. Genetics of bipolar affective disorder. *Curr Psychiatry Rep.* 2000 Apr;2(2):147-157.

13. Potash JB, Toolan J, Steele J, Miller EB, Pearl J, Zandi PP, Schulze TG, Kassem L, Simpson SG, Lopez V, MacKinnon DF, McMahon FJ. The bipolar disorder phenome database: a resource for genetic studies. *Am J Psychiatry.* 2007 Aug;164(8):1229-1237.

14. Soares JC, Mann JJ. The functional neuroanatomy of mood disorders. *J Psychiatr Res.* 1997 Jul-Aug;31(4):393-432.

15. Soares JC, Mann JJ. The anatomy of mood disorders--review of structural neuroimaging studies. *Biol Psychiatry.* 1997 Jan 1;41(1):86-106.

16. Gogtay N, Ordonez A, Herman DH, Hayashi KM, Greenstein D, Vaituzis C, Lenane M, Clasen L, Sharp W, Giedd JN, Jung D, Nugent Iii TF, Toga AW, Leibenluft E, Thompson PM, Rapoport JL. Dynamic mapping of cortical development before and after the onset of pediatric bipolar illness. *J Child Psychol Psychiatry.* 2007 Sep;48(9):852-862.

17. Hirschfeld RM. Psychiatric Management, from "Guideline Watch: Practice Guideline for the Treatment of Patients With Bipolar Disorder, 2nd Edition". http://www.psychiatryonline.com/content. aspx?aID=148440. Accessed on February 11, 2008.

18. Sachs GS, Printz DJ, Kahn DA, Carpenter D, Docherty JP. The Expert Consensus Guideline Series: Medication Treatment of Bipolar Disorder 2000. *Postgrad Med.* 2000 Apr;Spec No.:1-104.

19. Sachs GS, Thase ME. Bipolar disorder therapeutics: maintenance treatment. *Biol Psychiatry.* 2000 Sep 15;48(6):573-581.

20. Huxley NA, Parikh SV, Baldessarini RJ. Effectiveness of psychosocial treatments in bipolar disorder: state of the evidence. *Harv Rev Psychiatry.* 2000 Sep;8(3):126-140.

21. Miklowitz DJ. A review of evidence-based psychosocial interventions for bipolar disorder. *J Consult Clin Psychol.* 2006 67(Suppl 11):28-33.

22. Kupka RW, Nolen WA, Post RM, McElroy SL, Altshuler LL, Denicoff KD, Frye MA, Keck PE, Jr., Leverich GS, Rush AJ, Suppes T, Pollio C, Drexhage HA. High rate of autoimmune thyroiditis in bipolar disorder: lack of association with lithium exposure. *Biol Psychiatry.* 2002 Feb 15;51(4):305-311.

23. Bowden CL, Calabrese JR, McElroy SL, Gyulai L, Wassef A, Petty F, Pope HG, Jr., Chou JC, Keck PE, Jr., Rhodes LJ, Swann AC, Hirschfeld RM, Wozniak PJ, Group DMS. A randomized, placebo-controlled 12-month trial of divalproex and lithium in treatment of outpatients with bipolar I disorder. *Arch Gen Psychiatry.* 2000 May;57(5):481-489.

24. Calabrese JR, Shelton MD, Rapport DJ, Youngstrom EA, Jackson K, Bilali S, Ganocy SJ, Findling RL. A 20-month, double-blind, maintenance trial of lithium versus divalproex in rapid-cycling bipolar disorder. *Am J Psychiatry.* 2005 Nov;162(11):2152-2161.

25. Vainionpaa LK, Rattya J, Knip M, Tapanainen JS, Pakarinen AJ, Lanning P, Tekay A, Myllyla VV, Isojarvi JI. Valproate-induced hyperandrogenism during pubertal maturation in girls with epilepsy. *Ann Neurol.* 1999 Apr;45(4):444-450.

26. Joffe H, Cohen LS, Suppes T, McLaughlin WL, Lavori P, Adams JM, Hwang CH, Hall JE, Sachs GS. Valproate is associated with new-onset oligoamenorrhea with hyperandrogenism in women with bipolar disorder. *Biol Psychiatry.* 2006 Jun 1;59(11):1078-1086.

27. Joffe H, Cohen LS, Suppes T, Hwang CH, Molay F, Adams JM, Sachs GS, Hall JE. Longitudinal follow-up of reproductive and metabolic features of valproate-associated polycystic ovarian syndrome features: A preliminary report. *Biol Psychiatry.* 2006 Dec 15;60(12):1378-1381.

28. Tohen M, Sanger TM, McElroy SL, Tollefson GD, Chengappa KN, Daniel DG, Petty F, Centorrino F, Wang R, Grundy SL, Greaney MG, Jacobs TG, David SR, Toma V. Olanzapine versus placebo in the treatment of acute mania. Olanzapine HGEH Study Group. *Am J Psychiatry.* 1999 May;156(5):702-709.

29. Thase ME, Sachs GS. Bipolar depression: pharmacotherapy and related therapeutic strategies. *Biol Psychiatry.* 2000 Sep 15;48(6):558-572.

30. Sachs GS, Nierenberg AA, Calabrese JR, Marangell LB, Wisniewski SR, Gyulai L, Friedman ES, Bowden CL, Fossey MD, Ostacher MJ, Ketter TA, Patel J, Hauser P, Rapport D, Martinez JM, Allen MH, Miklowitz DJ, Otto MW, Dennehy EB, Thase ME. Effectiveness of adjunctive antidepressant treatment for bipolar depression. *N Engl J Med.* 2007 Apr 26;356(17):1711-1722.

31. MedlinePlus Drug Information: Lithium. http://www.nlm.nih.gov/medlineplus/druginfo/meds/a681039.html. Accessed on Nov 19, 2007.

32. MedlinePlus Drug Information: Carbamazepine. http://www.nlm. nih.gov/medlineplus/druginfo/meds/a682237.html. Accessed on July 13, 2007.

33. MedlinePlus Drug Information: Lamotrigine. http://www.nlm.nih. gov/medlineplus/druginfo/meds/a695007.html. Accessed on February 12, 2008.

34. MedlinePlus Drug Information: Valproic Acid. http://www.nlm.nih. gov/medlineplus/druginfo/meds/a682412.html. Accessed on February 12, 2008.

35. MedlinePlus Drug Information: Topiramate. http://www.nlm.nih. gov/medlineplus/druginfo/meds/a697012.html. Accessed on Febrary 22, 2008.

36. MedlinePlus Drug Information: Gabapentin. http://www.nlm.nih. gov/medlineplus/druginfo/meds/a694007.html. Accessed on February 22, 2008.

37. MedlinePlus Drug Information: Oxcarbazepine. http://www. nlm.nih.gov/medlineplus/druginfo/meds/a601245.html. Accessed on February 22, 2008.

38. Lieberman JA, Stroup TS, McEvoy JP, Swartz MS, Rosenheck RA, Perkins DO, Keefe RS, Davis SM, Davis CE, Lebowitz BD, Severe J, Hsiao JK. Effectiveness of antipsychotic drugs in patients with chronic schizophrenia. *N Engl J Med*. 2005 Sep 22;353(12):1209-1223.

39. Llewellyn A, Stowe ZN, Strader JR, Jr. The use of lithium and management of women with bipolar disorder during pregnancy and lactation. *J Consult Clin Psychol*. 1998 59(Suppl 6):57-64.

40. Viguera AC, Whitfield T, Baldessarini RJ, Newport J, Stowe Z, Reminick A, Zurick A, Cohen LS. Risk of recurrence in women with

bipolar disorder during pregnancy: prospective study of mood stabilizer discontinuation. *Am J Psychiatry.* 2007 Dec;164(12):1817-1824.

41. Yonkers KA, Wisner KL, Stowe Z, Leibenluft E, Cohen L, Miller L, Manber R, Viguera A, Suppes T, Altshuler L. Management of bipolar disorder during pregnancy and the postpartum period. *Am J Psychiatry.* 2004 Apr;161(4):608-620.

42. Miklowitz DJ, Otto MW, Frank E, Reilly-Harrington NA, Wisniewski SR, Kogan JN, Nierenberg AA, Calabrese JR, Marangell LB, Gyulai L, Araga M, Gonzalez JM, Shirley ER, Thase ME, Sachs GS. Psychosocial treatments for bipolar depression: a 1-year randomized trial from the Systematic Treatment Enhancement Program (STEP). *Arch Gen Psychiatry.* 2007 Apr;64(4):419-426.

43. Pandya M, Pozuelo L, Malone D. Electroconvulsive therapy: what the internist needs to know. *Cleve Clin J Med.* 2007 Sep;74(9):679-685.

44. *Mental Health: A Report of the Surgeon General.* U.S. Department of Health and Human Services, Substance Abuse and Mental Health Services Administration, Center for Mental Health Services, National Institutes of Health, National Institute of Mental Health. 1999.

45. Nierenberg AA, Burt T, Matthews J, Weiss AP. Mania associated with St. John's wort. *Biol Psychiatry.* 1999 Dec 15;46(12):1707-1708.

46. Henney JE. From the Food and Drug Administration: Risk of Drug Interactions With St John's Wort. *JAMA.* 2000 Apr 5;283(13):1679.

47. Stoll AL, Severus WE, Freeman MP, Rueter S, Zboyan HA, Diamond E, Cress KK, Marangell LB. Omega 3 fatty acids in bipolar disorder: a preliminary double-blind, placebo-controlled trial. *Arch Gen Psychiatry.* 1999 May;56(5):407-412.

48. Freeman MP, Hibbeln JR, Wisner KL, Davis JM, Mischoulon D, Peet M, Keck PE, Jr., Marangell LB, Richardson AJ, Lake J, Stoll AL.

Omega-3 fatty acids: evidence basis for treatment and future research in psychiatry. *J Consult Clin Psychol.* 2006 Dec;67(12):1954-1967.

49. Perlis RH, Ostacher MJ, Patel JK, Marangell LB, Zhang H, Wisniewski SR, Ketter TA, Miklowitz DJ, Otto MW, Gyulai L, Reilly-Harrington NA, Nierenberg AA, Sachs GS, Thase ME. Predictors of recurrence in bipolar disorder: primary outcomes from the Systematic Treatment Enhancement Program for Bipolar Disorder (STEP-BD). *Am J Psychiatry.* 2006 Feb;163(2):217-224.

50. Perlick DA, Rosenheck RA, Clarkin JF, Maciejewski PK, Sirey J, Struening E, Link BG. Impact of family burden and affective response on clinical outcome among patients with bipolar disorder. *Psychiatr Serv.* 2004 Sep;55(9):1029-1035.

For more information on bipolar disorder

Visit the National Library of Medicine's MedlinePlus, and En Español

For information on NIMH supported clinical trials, the Clinical trials at NIMH in Bethesda, MD or visit the National Library of Medicine Clinical Trials Database

Information from NIMH is available in multiple formats. You can browse online, download documents in PDF, and order materials through the mail. Check the NIMH Web site for the latest information on this topic and to order publications.

If you do not have Internet access please contact the NIMH Information Center at the numbers listed below.

National Institute of Mental Health
Science Writing, Press & Dissemination Branch
6001 Executive Boulevard

Room 8184, MSC 9663
Bethesda, MD 20892-9663
Phone: 301-443-4513 or
1-866-615-NIMH (6464) toll-free
TTY: 301-443-8431
TTY: 866-415-8051 toll-free
FAX: 301-443-4279
E-mail: nimhinfo@nih.gov
Web site: http://www.nimh.nih.gov

Reprints:

This publication is in the public domain and may be reproduced or copied without permission from NIMH. We encourage you to reproduce it and use it in your efforts to improve public health. Citation of the National Institute of Mental Health as a source is appreciated. However, using government materials inappropriately can raise legal or ethical concerns, so we ask you to use these guidelines:

- NIMH does not endorse or recommend any commercial products, processes, or services, and our publications may not be used for advertising or endorsement purposes.
- NIMH does not provide specific medical advice or treatment recommendations or referrals; our materials may not be used in a manner that has the appearance of such information.
- NIMH requests that non-Federal organizations not alter our publications in ways that will jeopardize the integrity and "brand" when using the publication.
- Addition of non-Federal Government logos and Web site links may not have the appearance of NIMH endorsement of any specific commercial products or services or medical treatments or services.

If you have questions regarding these guidelines and use of NIMH publications, please contact the NIMH Information Center at 1-866-615-6464 or e-mail at nimhinfo@nih.gov.

The photos in this publication are of models and are used for illustrative purposes only.

U.S. DEPARTMENT OF HEALTH AND HUMAN SERVICES
National Institutes of Health
NIH Publication 08-3679
Revised 2008

Share |

Options

- View the complete publication
- Download the PDF for the Web (31 page(s), 543 KBs)
- Order a hardcopy
- See all NIMH publications about: Bipolar Disorder
- Browse Mental Health Topics
- About NIMH Publications
- Contact Us
- Staff Directories
- Privacy Policy

Copyright